Lon

Tel: 0203

D0995159

CGP

Functional Skills
English

Edexcel – Entry Level 3

Getting ready for the Edexcel Entry Level 3 Functional Skills English test?
This fantastic CGP book covers everything you need... and nothing you don't!

Every topic is clearly explained, along with all the reading and writing skills you'll need.
There are plenty of questions to help build up your confidence, including two realistic
practice papers — with answers for everything at the back of the book.

CGP — still the best! ☺

Our sole aim here at CGP is to produce the highest quality books —
carefully written, immaculately presented and dangerously close to being funny.

Then we work our socks off to get them out to you
— at the cheapest possible prices.

Contents

Part 1 — Reading

Section One — Finding Information in Texts

Section Two — Advice for the Reading Test

The Reading Test

Part 2 — Writing

Section One — What to Write About

Section Two — Different Types of Writing

Section Three — Using Grammar

Section Four — Using Correct Punctuation

Section Five — Using Correct Spelling

Section Six — Advice for the Writing Test

The Writing Test

Published by CGP

Editors:
Izzy Bowen
Tom Carney
Heather Cowley
Becca Lakin
Rebecca Russell
James Summersgill
Sean Walsh

With thanks to Matt Topping and Susan Blanch for the proofreading.

With thanks to Ana Pungartnik for the copyright research.

All names, places and incidents are fictitious, any resemblance to actual events or persons is entirely coincidental.

ISBN: 978 1 78908 395 8

Printed by Elanders Ltd, Newcastle upon Tyne.
Clipart from Corel®

What is Functional Skills English?

Functional Skills are a set of qualifications

1) They are designed to give you the **skills** you need in **everyday life**.

2) There are **three** Functional Skills **subjects** — **English**, **Maths** and **ICT**.

3) You may have to sit **tests** in **one**, **two** or all **three** of these subjects.

4) Each subject has **five levels** — **Entry Level 1-3**, **Level 1** and **Level 2**.

This book is for Functional Skills English

1) There are **three** parts to Functional Skills English — **reading, writing** and **speaking, listening and communicating**.

2) To get a Functional Skills English qualification, you need to **pass all three parts**.

3) This book covers the **reading** and **writing** parts of **Functional English Entry Level 3**.

The papers for each exam board are slightly different — ask your teacher to make sure you know which one you're sitting.

There are two tests and one controlled assessment

1) **Speaking, listening and communicating** is tested by a **controlled assessment** in class.

2) **Reading** and **writing** are tested in **two separate tests**.

Reading

- In the test, you have to **read** a **range of texts** and **answer questions** on them.

- Some questions might be **multiple choice** (you choose the correct answer).

- Some questions might ask you to **write** your **answer**.

- You **don't** have to write in **full sentences**.

- You **won't** lose marks for **spelling, punctuation** or **grammar mistakes**.

Writing

- In the test, you will be asked to write **two texts** — e.g. a letter and an article.

- You **will lose marks** if your spelling, grammar and punctuation are **wrong**.

- There will also be questions on things like **plurals** and **alphabetical order**, as well as a **spelling** test.

How to Use this Book

This book summarises everything you need to know

1) This book is designed to help you **go over** what you are already learning in class.

2) Use it along with any **notes** and **resources** your teacher has given you.

3) You can work through this book from **start** to **finish**...

4) ...or you can just **target the topics** that you're **not sure** about.

Use this book to revise and test yourself

1) This book is split into **two parts** — **reading** and **writing**.

2) The topics in each part are usually **spread over two pages**.

Here is the title of the topic.

On the left-hand page there is all the important information for each topic.

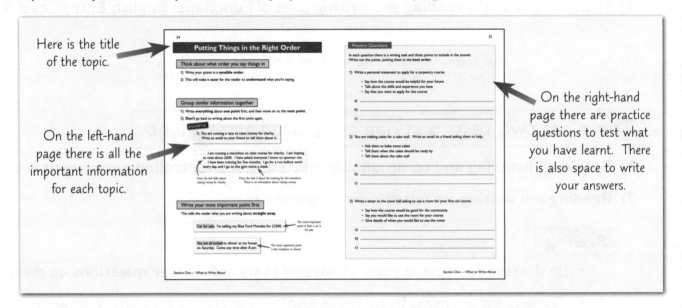

On the right-hand page there are practice questions to test what you have learnt. There is also space to write your answers.

There are answers to all the practice questions and the practice papers at the back of the book.

There's lots of test-style practice

1) There's a **practice paper** at the **end** of each part of the book.

2) These papers are based on **actual Functional Skills assessments**.

3) This means that the questions are **similar** to the ones you'll be asked in the **real tests**.

4) They are a good way of **testing** the **skills you've learnt** under **timed conditions**.

5) This will give you a **good idea** of what to expect when you come to take the real tests.

Using a Dictionary

You can use a dictionary in the reading paper

1) Some questions in the reading paper might suggest you use a **dictionary**.

2) You can use a dictionary to look up the **meaning** of a **tricky word** at any time in the reading paper.

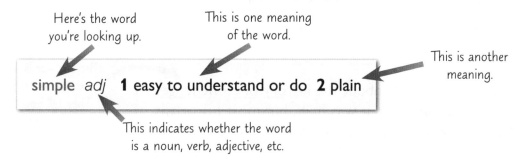

Here's the word you're looking up.

This is one meaning of the word.

This is another meaning.

simple *adj* **1** easy to understand or do **2** plain

This indicates whether the word is a noun, verb, adjective, etc.

Practise using a dictionary before the reading test

1) The words in a **dictionary** are listed in **alphabetical order**.

2) This means all the words starting with '**a**' are **grouped together** first, then all the words starting with '**b**', and so on.

3) Words that start with the **same letter** are listed in the order of their **second letter**. For example, '**r<u>a</u>ce**' comes **before** '**r<u>u</u>sh**'.

4) When you're looking for a word, check the words in **bold** at the **top** of **each page**.

5) These words help you work out which **page** you need to **turn to**.

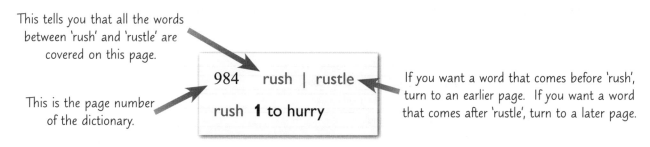

This tells you that all the words between 'rush' and 'rustle' are covered on this page.

This is the page number of the dictionary.

984   rush | rustle

rush **1** to hurry

If you want a word that comes before 'rush', turn to an earlier page. If you want a word that comes after 'rustle', turn to a later page.

Don't use a dictionary all the time

1) Dictionaries can be **helpful**, but **don't** use them **too often**.

2) Looking up **lots** of words will **slow you down** in the test.

3) If you're struggling with a word, look at the **rest of the sentence**. This is a good way of **working out** what the word could mean.

> If there's a word you don't recognise in this book, use a dictionary to look it up. It's a good way of practising.

Picking Out the Main Point

The main point of a text is what it is about

1) You **don't** need to read **all** of a text to find the **main point**.

2) Move your eyes **quickly** over the text, looking for **key words**.

3) **Key words** are the **most important** words in the text.

4) **Underline** any key words that you find.

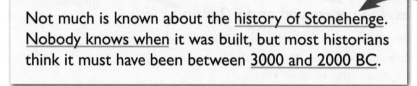

Not much is known about the <u>history of Stonehenge</u>. <u>Nobody knows when</u> it was built, but most historians think it must have been between <u>3000 and 2000 BC</u>.

The key words in the text are underlined. They tell you that the text is about the history of Stonehenge.

Taking <u>regular exercise helps</u> to keep you <u>healthy</u>. It <u>reduces your risk</u> of heart disease and diabetes.

The key words tell you that the text is about why exercise is good for you.

The most important point usually comes first

1) Some texts are divided into **paragraphs**. Paragraphs are **groups** of sentences.

2) The **main point** of a text is often in the **first paragraph**.

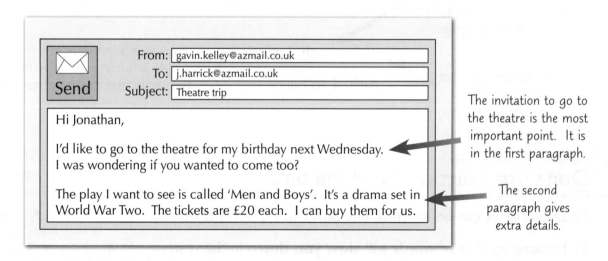

From: gavin.kelley@azmail.co.uk
To: j.harrick@azmail.co.uk
Subject: Theatre trip

Send

Hi Jonathan,

I'd like to go to the theatre for my birthday next Wednesday. I was wondering if you wanted to come too?

The play I want to see is called 'Men and Boys'. It's a drama set in World War Two. The tickets are £20 each. I can buy them for us.

The invitation to go to the theatre is the most important point. It is in the first paragraph.

The second paragraph gives extra details.

Practice Questions

Read each text below, and then answer the question next to it. Circle your answer.

Blue River

Members-only swimming club

Blue River is an exclusive swimming club in Tunaley. Our facilities include:

- A 50-metre swimming pool
- A bubble pool and steam room
- Sports massage

Open 7 am to 10 pm every day.

1) This text is about:

    a)   A swimming club

    b)   Sports massage

    c)   Swimming lessons

    d)   Tunaley

GET ON YOUR BIKE

Cycling is a great way to get around. The best things about cycling are:
- It's free
- It's good for the environment
- It's good exercise

There are lots of ways to get involved in cycling. Look out for a local cycling club in your town or go out with a friend. Don't forget to wear a helmet!

2) This text:

    a)   Tells you about cycling helmets

    b)   Persuades you to do more exercise

    c)   Tells you about cycling

    d)   Advertises a cycling club

Cleaner Wanted

Family looking for an experienced cleaner for a large 5-bedroom house in West Tranby. Duties to include:

- General household cleaning
- Ironing
- Laundry

4 hours per week. Pay from £11 an hour depending on experience. References required.
Please contact Mrs Anita Rao on **0141 496 0154**.

3) This text:

    a)   Tells you about Anita Rao

    b)   Advertises a cleaning job

    c)   Advertises a house for sale

    d)   Tells you about West Tranby

INTER-COFFEE

George Street, Handelby

We have 12 computers with high-speed internet, plus free Wi-Fi for all our customers.

Coffee, cake and snacks served all day.

Open 8 am to 11 pm Monday to Saturday.

4) This text is about:

    a)   The internet

    b)   George Street

    c)   A restaurant

    d)   An internet café

Using Key Words to Find Information

Look for key words in the question and the text

1) You **don't** have to read the **whole text** to find a piece of information.

2) Underline the **key words** in the **question**.

3) Quickly **read** through the text, looking for these **key words**.

4) When you find one, read the rest of the sentence **carefully** to find the answer.

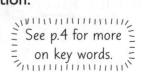

See p.4 for more on key words.

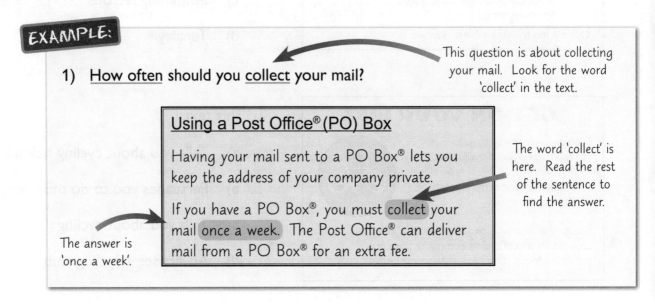

EXAMPLE:

1) How often should you collect your mail?

This question is about collecting your mail. Look for the word 'collect' in the text.

Using a Post Office® (PO) Box

Having your mail sent to a PO Box® lets you keep the address of your company private.

If you have a PO Box®, you must collect your mail once a week. The Post Office® can deliver mail from a PO Box® for an extra fee.

The word 'collect' is here. Read the rest of the sentence to find the answer.

The answer is 'once a week'.

Think about what the question means

The key words in the **question** might not be **exactly** the same as the words in the **text**.

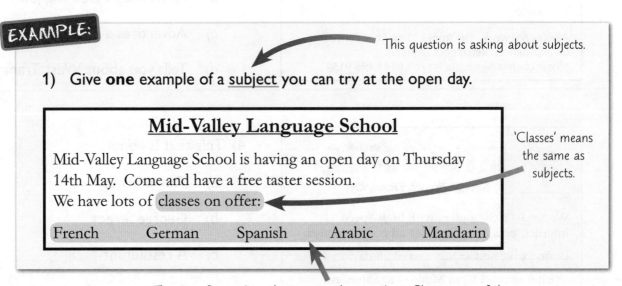

EXAMPLE:

1) Give **one** example of a subject you can try at the open day.

This question is asking about subjects.

Mid-Valley Language School

Mid-Valley Language School is having an open day on Thursday 14th May. Come and have a free taster session.
We have lots of classes on offer:

French   German   Spanish   Arabic   Mandarin

'Classes' means the same as subjects.

There are five options that answer the question. Choose one of them.

Read the text below, and then answer the questions underneath.

FRIDAY 18th JULY — TARNFORD GAZETTE

Upper Tarnford to get bypass

Traffic has been increasing in Upper Tarnford over the last 5 years. Now the council have decided to build a bypass around the town. The council hope a bypass will reduce traffic problems in the area.

Upper Tarnford town centre is often full of cars and lorries. The roads are particularly busy at rush hour. Most of the traffic is passing through from Kellingworth to Lower Tarnford. The new bypass would mean people could drive past Upper Tarnford rather than through it.

Some people are worried that the bypass will affect the environment. It will cut through a large part of Pavey Wood. This area is very popular with birdwatchers because it is home to a rare type of sparrow.

Construction of the bypass is due to begin in September. It will take 6 months to complete.

What do you think about the bypass? Visit our website today and have your say.

1) How long has the traffic been increasing in Upper Tarnford? Circle your answer.

   a) The last 3 years　　　c) Since September

   b) The last 5 years　　　d) The last 6 months

2) Who has decided to build the bypass? Circle your answer.

   a) Local people　　　c) The council

   b) Car drivers　　　d) Birdwatchers

3) When will the building of the bypass start?

....

4) When is the traffic in Upper Tarnford at its worst?

....

5) You want to give your opinion about the bypass. What should you do?

....

....

Working Out Tricky Words

A dictionary can help you find out what tricky words mean

1) If you want to know the meaning of a word, one way is to use a **dictionary**.

2) Some dictionaries give **more than one** meaning for each word. You might only need **one**.

There's more about how to use a dictionary on p.3.

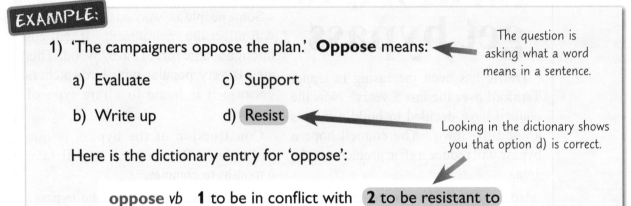

EXAMPLE:

1) 'The campaigners oppose the plan.' **Oppose** means:

   a) Evaluate   c) Support

   b) Write up   d) Resist

The question is asking what a word means in a sentence.

Looking in the dictionary shows you that option d) is correct.

Here is the dictionary entry for 'oppose':

oppose *vb* **1** to be in conflict with **2** to be resistant to

You can also look around the word

Looking at the rest of the **sentence** can sometimes help you **work out** what a word means.

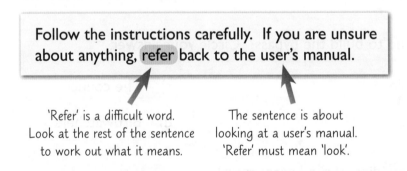

Follow the instructions carefully. If you are unsure about anything, refer back to the user's manual.

'Refer' is a difficult word. Look at the rest of the sentence to work out what it means.

The sentence is about looking at a user's manual. 'Refer' must mean 'look'.

Use word types to help you to find a word's meaning

1) Word types include **nouns**, **verbs** and **adjectives**.

2) Knowing the word type of a tricky word can give you a **clue** to what it means.

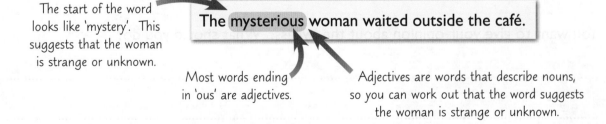

The start of the word looks like 'mystery'. This suggests that the woman is strange or unknown.

The mysterious woman waited outside the café.

Most words ending in 'ous' are adjectives.

Adjectives are words that describe nouns, so you can work out that the word suggests the woman is strange or unknown.

Working Out Tricky Words

Choose the method that seems best

1) You can use **any** of these methods to help you find a **word's meaning**.

2) Looking at the rest of the sentence can sometimes be **quicker** than using a dictionary.

3) But, if you're still **not sure** what the word means, **check** a **dictionary**.

Practice Questions

Read the text below, and then answer the questions underneath.

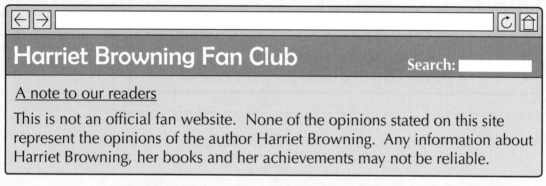

Harriet Browning Fan Club

Search:

A note to our readers

This is not an official fan website. None of the opinions stated on this site represent the opinions of the author Harriet Browning. Any information about Harriet Browning, her books and her achievements may not be reliable.

1) Use a dictionary to look up the word **'official'**. Write down what it means.

....

....

2) Read the sentence starting 'None of the opinions...'
   Which word in this sentence means **'said'**? Circle your answer.

   a) Opinions   c) Represent

   b) Stated   d) Author

3) What type of word is **'achievements'**? Circle your answer.

   a) Noun   c) Adjective

   b) Verb   d) Pronoun

4) What is the meaning of the word **'reliable'**? You can use any method that seems best.

....

....

Identifying the Purpose of Texts

Texts have different purposes

1) A text is a **piece of writing**. Every text has a **purpose**.

2) The **purpose** is the reason **why** the text has been written.

3) For example, a **leaflet** might give you **information** about something.

4) A **recipe** or a **manual** might **instruct** you on how to do something.

> <u>Setting Up Your PC</u>
> 1. Find a suitable spot for your PC.
> 2. Plug in the PC.
> 3. Attach the monitor, keyboard and mouse.
> 4. Turn on the computer and follow the instructions onscreen.

This text instructs you on how to set up a computer.

Read the text closely to see what its purpose is

When reading a text, look out for **key details** that give you **clues** about its purpose.

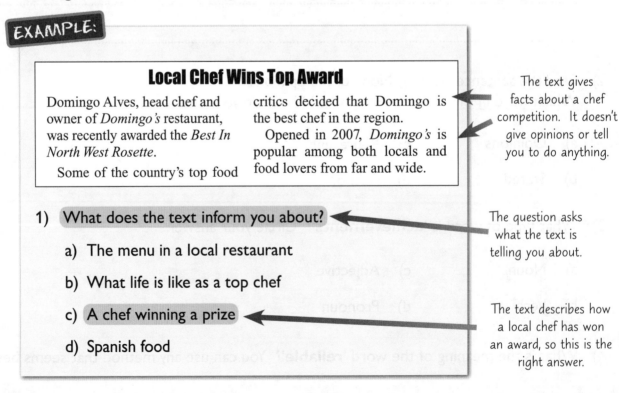

EXAMPLE:

Local Chef Wins Top Award

Domingo Alves, head chef and owner of *Domingo's* restaurant, was recently awarded the *Best In North West Rosette*.

Some of the country's top food critics decided that Domingo is the best chef in the region.

Opened in 2007, *Domingo's* is popular among both locals and food lovers from far and wide.

The text gives facts about a chef competition. It doesn't give opinions or tell you to do anything.

1) What does the text inform you about?

   a) The menu in a local restaurant

   b) What life is like as a top chef

   c) A chef winning a prize

   d) Spanish food

The question asks what the text is telling you about.

The text describes how a local chef has won an award, so this is the right answer.

Read each text below, and then answer the question underneath it.

> ## Being an on-call firefighter
>
> Working as an on-call firefighter is difficult, but it can also be very fun and rewarding.
>
> On-call firefighters are ordinary people who are trained to respond to incidents. They are on call for several hours a week, and need to be ready to deal with any emergencies that occur during that time.
>
> These on-call firefighters assist their local community and even help save lives. In return, they receive a small amount of money for their service. Not just anyone can become an on-call firefighter, though — you have to be at least 18 years old and pass a number of health checks.

1) The purpose of the text is to inform. What does the text inform you about?

   a) A recent fire in a town   c) Working as a on-call firefighter

   b) How to put a fire out   d) How to prevent fires

> ## Double Chocolate Chunk Cookies
>
> ### Ingredients
>
> | | |
> |---|---|
> | 170 g plain flour | 180g golden caster sugar |
> | 30 g cocoa powder | 1/2 tsp salt |
> | 160 g unsalted butter | 150g dark chocolate chunks |
>
> ### Method
>
> 1. Preheat the oven to 160 °C and line a baking tray with greaseproof paper.
> 2. Beat the butter and sugar together until the mixture turns pale and fluffy.
> 3. Mix in the flour, cocoa powder, salt and chocolate until a dough forms.
> 4. Divide the dough into 24 equal balls. Flatten each one slightly.
> 5. Place the cookies on the tray six at a time and bake for 12 minutes.

2) What is the purpose of this text?

   a) To give a description of a cookie   c) To give cookie-making instructions

   b) To narrate a story about cookies   d) To convince you to make cookies

Using Layout to Find Information

Use subheadings to help you find information

1) **Subheadings** are titles in the text that tell you what each **section** is **about**.

2) Look for **subheadings** that **match** the information you need.

3) **Read** the **text** under that **subheading**. The **answer** will probably be there.

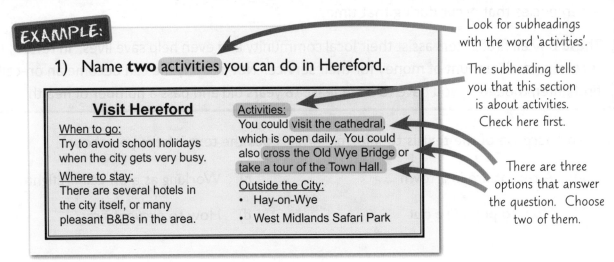

EXAMPLE:

1) Name **two** activities you can do in Hereford.

Visit Hereford

When to go:
Try to avoid school holidays when the city gets very busy.

Where to stay:
There are several hotels in the city itself, or many pleasant B&Bs in the area.

Activities:
You could visit the cathedral, which is open daily. You could also cross the Old Wye Bridge or take a tour of the Town Hall.

Outside the City:
• Hay-on-Wye
• West Midlands Safari Park

Look for subheadings with the word 'activities'.

The subheading tells you that this section is about activities. Check here first.

There are three options that answer the question. Choose two of them.

Bullet points can help you find information

They **separate** information so it is **easier** to **read**.

EXAMPLE:

1) Give **two** ways of contacting Tiger Jewels.

If you have a complaint, please contact us by:
• Emailing our Customer Complaints Centre
• Telephoning our Customer Complaints Helpline

These are the two answers to the question. The bullet points make them easier to spot.

Words might be written in bold or in capital letters

This makes **important** information **stand out**.

Helmets and protective clothing MUST be worn at all times when inside the paintballing arena. **Do not** remove your helmet until you have left the arena.

This is important. It is in capital letters so it stands out.

This is in bold so you notice it when you are reading the sentence.

Using Layout to Find Information

Sometimes the answer will be in a table

Use the **column headings** to help you find the information.

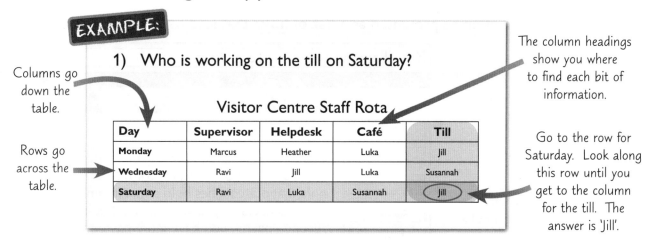

EXAMPLE:

1) Who is working on the till on Saturday?

Columns go down the table.

Rows go across the table.

Visitor Centre Staff Rota

Day	Supervisor	Helpdesk	Café	Till
Monday	Marcus	Heather	Luka	Jill
Wednesday	Ravi	Jill	Luka	Susannah
Saturday	Ravi	Luka	Susannah	Jill

The column headings show you where to find each bit of information.

Go to the row for Saturday. Look along this row until you get to the column for the till. The answer is 'Jill'.

Contents help you find the right page

1) The contents is a **list** of the **sections** in a book.

2) The **page numbers** of each section are given so you can find the section you need.

Depending on the book, contents might also list page titles or topics.

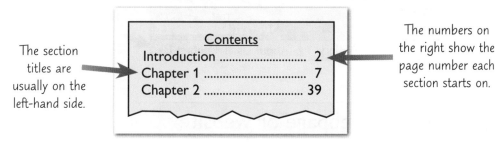

Contents

Introduction 2
Chapter 1 7
Chapter 2 39

The section titles are usually on the left-hand side.

The numbers on the right show the page number each section starts on.

An index is a list of key topics

1) An **index** lists a text's **main topics** in **alphabetical order**.

2) It's usually found at the **back** or **end** of a text.

Turn to the back of this book to see its index.

3) You can use an index to find out which **pages** have information about a topic.

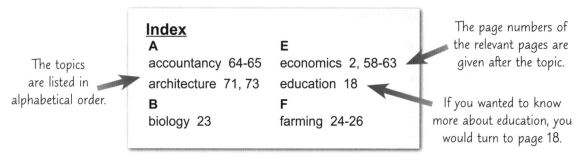

Index

A
accountancy 64-65
architecture 71, 73
B
biology 23

E
economics 2, 58-63
education 18
F
farming 24-26

The topics are listed in alphabetical order.

The page numbers of the relevant pages are given after the topic.

If you wanted to know more about education, you would turn to page 18.

Using Layout to Find Information

Menus and tabs help you to navigate websites

1) Most websites have a **menu** telling you what the different sections of the site **are about**.

2) The menu will often be presented as a **list** of **links** that lead to different webpages.

The menu on this website includes links to different pages of the website.

The webpage you're currently on will often be made clear in the menu — the different colour here tells you that you are on 'Costs'.

3) Sometimes websites use **tabs** instead of a menu.

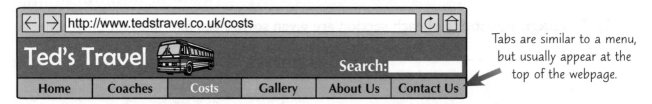

Tabs are similar to a menu, but usually appear at the top of the webpage.

Links take you to another webpage or website

1) Clicking a link on a website takes you to a **different page** on the website, or to a completely **different website**.

2) Links might be a **different colour** or **underlined**.

The different colour and the underlining shows that this is a link.

This link will take you to a different part of the website.

Read the text below, and then answer the questions underneath.

Wallsea Birdwatching Cruises

"A wonderful experience! We saw so many different birds, and our children loved it."

Home	Tours	Wildlife	Our Crew	Donate	Contact

A Wallsea Birdwatching Cruise is a perfect family day out. Children will enjoy the **beautiful coastline** and **interesting wildlife**. Birds that are often seen include:

- Puffins
- Fulmars
- Arctic terns
- Sea eagles
- Gannets
- Razorbills

Tour Times

Cruises run throughout the summer. See table for times.

Months	Daily departure times			
June		11.30 am	1.30 pm	
July	10.00 am	11.30 am	3.00 pm	
August	10.00 am	12.00 pm	2.00 pm	4.00 pm

ALL PASSENGERS MUST WEAR LIFE JACKETS

1) Which **one** of these statements is correct? Circle your answer.

a) The cruise doesn't run in June.

b) There are only afternoon cruises in June.

c) You can take a cruise at 11.30 in June.

d) July has more cruises than August.

2) Why does the writer use capital letters to tell passengers they must wear life jackets?

....

....

3) Give **two** things children will enjoy on a Wallsea Birdwatching Cruise.

1 ....

2 ....

4) Circle **two** ways you could find out more about wildlife.

a) Donate to the company

b) Click the 'Wildlife' tab

c) Read the table

d) Click the link on the word 'wildlife'

Different Types of Question

You might have to choose the right answer from a list

1) For some questions, you will be given a **right** answer and some **wrong** ones.

2) Look at each option **carefully**.

3) **Rule out** the options that are **definitely wrong** until you are left with the **right answer**.

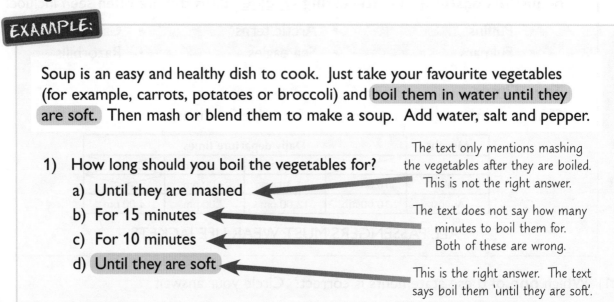

EXAMPLE:

Soup is an easy and healthy dish to cook. Just take your favourite vegetables (for example, carrots, potatoes or broccoli) and boil them in water until they are soft. Then mash or blend them to make a soup. Add water, salt and pepper.

1) How long should you boil the vegetables for?
   a) Until they are mashed
   b) For 15 minutes
   c) For 10 minutes
   d) Until they are soft

The text only mentions mashing the vegetables after they are boiled. This is not the right answer.

The text does not say how many minutes to boil them for. Both of these are wrong.

This is the right answer. The text says boil them 'until they are soft'.

You might have to write down your own answer

1) **Read** the question **carefully** and work out what information it is asking for.

2) **Find** that information in the text and **write** it in the space you are given.

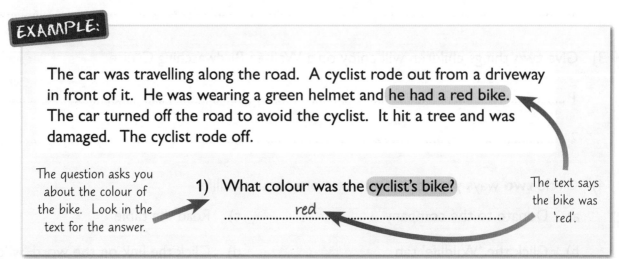

EXAMPLE:

The car was travelling along the road. A cyclist rode out from a driveway in front of it. He was wearing a green helmet and he had a red bike. The car turned off the road to avoid the cyclist. It hit a tree and was damaged. The cyclist rode off.

The question asks you about the colour of the bike. Look in the text for the answer.

1) What colour was the cyclist's bike?
   .... red ....

The text says the bike was 'red'.

Different Types of Question

You might need to use a dictionary

1) Some questions will ask you to give the **meaning** of a word.

2) You can use a **dictionary** to help you find the meaning.

3) The options given in the question might not match the definition in your dictionary **exactly**. Pick the **closest** option.

Look at pages 8-9 for other ways to work out the meaning of a word.

EXAMPLE:

Thousands of people have had solar panels installed on their property. Many of these customers are already seeing a return on their investment.

1) You may use a dictionary to answer this question.
Investment means:
   a) Someone who installs solar panels
   b) A type of solar panel
   c) A type of roof
   d) A sum of money

a), b) and c) definitely don't match the dictionary entry.

Option d) is the closest to the dictionary entry.

investment *noun*
1 an amount of money put into something for profit

This is the dictionary entry for 'investment'.

Some questions could ask you to replace words

1) You might be asked to choose a word that could **replace** another word.

2) The **meaning** of the sentence should stay they same.

3) Work out the meaning of the word you need to **replace** first.

4) Then choose the option which has the **closest** meaning.

EXAMPLE:

Valery remained composed during the trial.

1) You may use a dictionary to answer this question.
The word **composed** could best be replaced with:
   a) Calm
   b) Upset
   c) Impatient
   d) Silent

Option a) has the closest meaning to 'composed'.

Options b), c) and d) do not mean the same thing as 'composed'.

composed *adj*
1 in control of your emotions; calm; collected

This is the dictionary entry for 'composed'.

Reading Test Advice

Read the text carefully

1) Read the **whole text** before you answer the questions.

2) Make sure you understand **what the text is about**.

3) **Look up** tricky words if you need to.

Some words in the reading texts could be from the word list (see p.113-114). Learn what these words mean before your test so you understand them on the day.

This text is a job advert for a receptionist.

You could use your dictionary to look up words like 'exceptional'.

> We are a law firm looking for a receptionist to join our Birmingham office. You must have previous experience and exceptional communication skills. To apply, please send a CV to the address below.

Read the question carefully

1) Make sure you understand **what the question is asking** before you answer it.

2) Look **back at the text** to check your answer before you write it down.

> 1) What city would the receptionist be working in?

This question is asking for the name of a city. Look back at the text to check where the receptionist job is. The answer is 'Birmingham'.

Follow the instructions

1) The question always tells you **what you need to do**.

2) **Underline** the **important words** to make it easier to follow the instructions.

3) Check **how many marks** each question is worth so you know **how much to write**.

> 2) List two things somebody applying for this job must have.
>
> (2 marks)

There are two marks, so you need to write two different things — 'previous experience' and 'exceptional communication skills'.

Reading Test Advice

Answer as many questions as you can

1) You have **45 minutes** to do the reading test, and there are **24 marks** in total.

2) If you can't do a question, **leave it** and **move on** to the next one.

3) You can **come back** to the questions you have left if you have time at the end.

4) If you finish early, **check your answers**.

5) Read the questions again. Make sure what you have written **answers** the question.

Don't worry too much about spelling

1) **Don't worry** if you are not sure how to spell a word.

2) Your spelling **will not** be marked in the reading test.

3) You just need to make sure that what you write can be **understood**.

4) Make sure your handwriting is **clear**.

You don't need to write in full sentences

1) In the reading test, you **will not** get marks for writing in **full sentences**.

2) Just write enough to **answer the question**.

EXAMPLE:

> The council have started a new rubbish-collection scheme. All houses in the area have been given a new bin and recycling boxes. The recycling is collected every week and the rubbish is collected every other week. The scheme has been running for five weeks. It is very popular so far.
>
> 1) How long has the rubbish-collection scheme been running for?
>
> .... *five weeks* ....

You can just write one or two words for your answer. You don't need to write a sentence.

BLANK PAGE

Candidate Surname	Candidate Forename(s)

Date	Candidate Signature

Functional Skills

English   Entry Level 3

Reading

Time allowed: 45 minutes

You **may** use a dictionary.

Instructions to candidates
- Use **black or blue ink** to write your answers.
- Write your name and the date in the box above.
- Answer each question in the space provided.
- Some questions should be answered by ticking a box.

Information for candidates
- There are **24 marks** available for this paper.
- The marks available for each question are given in brackets.

Advice to candidates
- Read all the questions carefully.
- If you have time, check your answers at the end.

Total Marks

Read Text A, then answer Questions 1 - 6.

Text A

Grow Your Own Herbs

Many people enjoy cooking with herbs. Growing your own is much cheaper than buying them in the supermarket. Herbs like thyme and parsley are popular because they are very easy to grow indoors.

Position your herbs in a bright place so that they receive plenty of sunlight.

You will need:

- a plant pot
- compost
- seeds

Method

1) Fill your pot with compost until it is about three-quarters full.

2) Sprinkle a thin layer of seeds on top.

3) Place enough compost on top of your seeds to cover them.

4) Water your seeds regularly and wait for them to grow.

Hints

Make sure your herbs have sufficient water, but don't over-water them.

Some herbs grow all year round, but others stop growing in autumn and winter.

Check the back of the seed packet to find the best time to plant them. You can also find this information on gardening websites.

Tick the correct box.

1 What is the **main** purpose of this text?

☐ **A** To encourage you to grow vegetables   ☐ **C** To advertise compost

☐ **B** To tell you how to grow herbs   ☐ **D** To teach you how to cook

(1 mark)

2 According to Text A, where should you keep your plant pots?

☐ **A** In a cool place   ☐ **C** In a dark place

☐ **B** In a bright place   ☐ **D** In a warm place

(1 mark)

3 **You can use a dictionary for this question.**

'Make sure your herbs have **sufficient** water'. What does the word **sufficient** mean?

☐ **A** Chilled   ☐ **C** Enough

☐ **B** Constant   ☐ **D** Tropical

(1 mark)

Write your answer on the lines provided.

4 How much compost should you put on top of your seeds?

....

(1 mark)

5 Name **two** herbs that the text says are easy to grow.

1 ....

2 ....

(2 marks)

6 You want to know the best time to plant your seeds.
Which **two** places does the text suggest you should look?

1 ....

2 ....

(2 marks)

Read Text B, then answer Questions 7 - 12.

Text B

MOVE E-Z

We appreciate that moving house or flat can be very stressful. Here at Move E-Z we provide everything you need to make moving a breeze.

SERVICES INCLUDE:

- **Helping you pack up**
- **Cleaning your old property**
- **Unpacking in your new home**

EXPERIENCED COMPANY

Our staff are careful, thorough and supportive, so there is nothing for you to worry about. We listen to your needs and use our expert knowledge to give you the best service available. You can be sure that all your items will be packed safely and everything will arrive intact. We guarantee that if anything is damaged during the move, we will replace it for you as quickly as possible.

We will take on any job, but we are especially good at helping elderly people move.

PRICING

To arrange a free inspection of your property, call us on **0909 8790375**, email us at **move_ez@azmail.co.uk**, or visit our office at Edenbrook Industrial Estate. We can provide a quote for any job within two working days. This quote will include all costs, so there will be no nasty surprises.

Making moving E-Z

7 According to Text B, which **one** of the statements below is true?

☐ **A** The company only helps elderly people.

☐ **B** Inspection takes three working days.

☐ **C** Quotes include all costs.

☐ **D** Move E-Z staff are careless.

(1 mark)

8 What type of move does Move E-Z say they are best at?

☐ **A** Big moves

☐ **B** House moves

☐ **C** Moves for old people

☐ **D** Small moves

(1 mark)

9 According to Text B, what will Move E-Z do if they damage anything?

☐ **A** Give you money for the item

☐ **B** Replace the item

☐ **C** Repair the item

☐ **D** Apologise

(1 mark)

10 **You can use a dictionary for this question.**

'everything will arrive intact.' **Intact** means:

☐ **A** Quickly

☐ **B** Wrapped up

☐ **C** Slowly

☐ **D** Undamaged

(1 mark)

11 You want to arrange an inspection. Give **three** ways of contacting Move E-Z.

1 ....

2 ....

3 ....

(3 marks)

12 Give **one** word that Move E-Z use to describe their staff.

....

(1 mark)

Read Text C, then answer Questions 13 - 17.

Text C

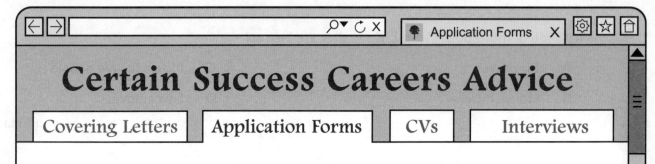

Certain Success Careers Advice

| Covering Letters | **Application Forms** | CVs | Interviews |

**Filling in a job application form can be difficult.
Here is some advice to help you.**

Basic Checklist

1) Read the instructions first. Some forms may ask you to use black ink.

2) Send everything you are asked for. For example, you might be asked to include a photograph of yourself.

3) Answer all the questions.

4) Make sure you spell everything right, especially the company's name.

5) Get a friend or family member to check your application.

Following this checklist will help you avoid any basic mistakes.
It will also help you to make a good first impression.

Experience and Personal Skills

There are lots of skills you might have, even if you have not worked for a while. You might have developed personal skills outside of work. For example, if you play football, you might be good at teamwork.

References

References are statements from other people describing your character. You could ask your most recent employer, a teacher or a tutor. Remember to ask their permission first.

13 What does this webpage help you to do?

☐ **A**   Fill in an application form   ☐ **C**   Write a reference

☐ **B**   Find a job   ☐ **D**   Write a CV

(1 mark)

14 **You can use a dictionary for this question.**

'References are statements from other people describing your character.'

Which word could best replace the word **character** in the sentence above?

☐ **A**   Hobbies   ☐ **C**   Family

☐ **B**   Job   ☐ **D**   Personality

(1 mark)

15 You are about to fill in a job application form.
What does the text say you should do first?

....

(1 mark)

16 Give **two** reasons why you should follow the checklist when applying for a job.

1 ....

2 ....

(2 marks)

17 You need a reference for your application.
List **three** people that the text suggests you could ask for a reference.

1 ....

2 ....

3 ....

(3 marks)

Total for paper = 24 marks

Who You Are Writing to and Why

Read the question carefully

1) It will tell you **who** you are writing to.

2) It will also tell you **why** you are writing to them.

3) You can **use** this information when you write your **answer**.

You need to know who you are writing to

This will tell you what kind of **language** to use.

Write a piece for your local newspaper about the opening of a new hospital.

You are writing to the people who read that newspaper.

Write an email to your friend to invite them to the cinema with you next week.

You are writing to your friend.

You need to know why you are writing

This will tell you **what** to write **about**.

Write an advert for an online auction site to sell your bike.

You are writing to give people information about your bike. You need to give details about it.

Write your personal statement for this job.

You are writing to tell the company why they should give you the job. You need to write about your skills and work experience.

Practice Questions

1) For each of these writing tasks, write down **who** you are writing to.

    a) Write a letter to the council to tell them about problems in your area.

        Who are you writing to? ....

    b) You are doing a charity bike ride. Write an email to your friends to tell them about it.

        Who are you writing to? ....

    c) Write a letter to your electricity supplier to complain about their new prices.

        Who are you writing to? ....

    d) You are organising the work Christmas party and need to invite the whole company.
        Write an email to tell everyone what you have arranged.

        Who are you writing to? ....

2) For each of these writing tasks, write down **why** you are writing.

    a) You want to paint your house. Write an email to your landlord to ask him if you can.

        Why are you writing? ....

    b) You need sponsorship for your charity swim.
        Write a note for the notice board at work, telling people how to sponsor you.

        Why are you writing? ....

    c) Your flight home was delayed. Write a complaint on the airline's webpage.

        Why are you writing? ....

    d) Write a letter to your local playgroup offering to volunteer once a week.

        Why are you writing? ....

Writing for Different Purposes and People

The purpose of a text is important

1) The purpose of a text is the reason **why** you're writing it.

2) There are lots of different purposes — to **inform**, **instruct**, **advise** and more.

3) The style of writing you use will depend on both **who** you are writing to and **why**.

4) For example, you wouldn't use the same language to **advise a friend** as you would to **advise a manager** at work.

Sometimes you write to people you know

1) Use more **chatty language** when you write to people you **know**.

2) For example, you might have to write to your **friends** or **family**.

3) Chatty language sounds more **personal** and **friendly**.

Hi Kate,
Crete was absolutely awesome. You should definitely go.
We had a fantastic time and the kids loved every second of it.

When writing to a friend, you use more chatty language.

You can use slang when you know the person you're writing to.
For example, the slang 'kids' instead of 'children'.

Sometimes you write to people you don't know

1) Use **serious** language when you write to people you **don't know**.

2) You should also use it for people you know who are **important**, like your boss at work.

3) Serious writing **sounds** more **professional**.

Dear Mrs Harris,

Crete is a very popular destination for a family holiday. I would recommend that you and your children consider visiting this year.

When you write to somebody you don't know, you use more serious language.

When writing to people you don't know, don't use slang.
For example, write 'children' instead of 'kids'.

Practice Questions

For each writing task there are two options for how to start the answer.
Choose the one that **sounds best** for each task, and circle its letter.

1) Write a letter to thank a relative for a present they gave you.

   a)   Hi Aunt Milly, I love the beautiful photo album you sent me. Thanks so much.

   b)   Dear Mrs Samson, I am writing to thank you for the photo album I received.

2) Write a personal statement to apply for a job as a childcare assistant.

   a)   I really want to have this job. I am brilliant with kids, so I would be a great choice.

   b)   I am applying for the childcare assistant position. I have lots of childcare experience.

3) Write an email to your manager asking for two weeks off.

   a)   Dear John, I would like to request two weeks of annual leave at the end of August.

   b)   Hi John, I'm off on my hols in Spain soon. Can you sort out some leave for me?

4) You were too busy to contact your friend at the weekend. Write an email to apologise.

   a)   Dear Mr Kent, I would like to apologise for not contacting you this weekend.

   b)   Hi Dave, I'm so sorry I didn't get in touch this weekend.

For each question below, underline the purpose of the writing task. Then circle 'chatty'
or 'serious' to show which kind of language you should use to complete each task.

5) An email to invite people to your friend's party.   chatty / serious

6) A letter to complain about your recent hotel stay.   chatty / serious

7) A leaflet to advertise your cleaning business.   chatty / serious

8) An email to ask your landlord to fix your gate.   chatty / serious

9) A letter to inform your grandma about your holiday.   chatty / serious

What to Include in Your Writing

Use the bullet points for ideas about what to write

1) You will usually be given **bullet points** underneath the writing task.

2) They will tell you **what** to write about.

EXAMPLE:

1) You are organising a charity day. Write an article telling people what will be happening.

You should include:

- Where it will be
- What events will be held
- What it is raising money for.

You need to write about these things.

You might have to make up some details

1) You can use details from the **question** in your writing.

2) You will probably need to **make up** some sensible details.

EXAMPLE:

1) You are unhappy with the service you have received from your mobile phone network. Write a letter asking to cancel your phone contract.

You should include:

- Why you are writing
- Why you are unhappy
- When you would like your contract to end.

You know this from the question. You are writing to cancel your phone contract.

You need to make up details here. For example, as soon as possible or at the end of the month.

You need to make up details here. For example, you have poor signal or you can never get through to customer services.

Practice Questions

Each question below has a writing task and four ideas about what to include.
Choose the writing that gives the **best answer** to the task, and circle its letter.

1) Write an advert to sell your bookshelf.

    You should include:
    • A description of the bookshelf
    • How much you are selling it for.

    a) Bookshelf for sale. It's two metres tall
        and made of oak. It's a great deal at £30.

    b) Bookshelf for sale. A desk, an armchair
        and a coffee table are also available.

    c) Furniture on sale for £40. Contact
        linda@azmail.co.uk for more details.

    d) Furniture for sale. It's five feet
        tall and made of black plastic.

2) Your train was 20 minutes late. Write a letter of complaint to the train company.

    You should include:
    • How the delay affected you
    • What you want them to do about it.

    a) Your trains are very dirty. I think you
        should clean the carriages more often.

    b) The standard of service on your trains is
        terrible. I now drive to work if possible.

    c) Yesterday, a late train made me
        late for work. I would like a refund.

    d) Your trains are always late. They
        often make me late for appointments.

3) Write a letter to the council to suggest an improvement to your area.

    You should include:
    • What improvement you think they should make
    • Why they should make this improvement.

    a) There are lots of problems in this area.
        Please make some improvements.

    b) The main road needs resurfacing. It is a
        busy road, and there are many potholes.

    c) I am not happy with the potholes
        on the streets in the town centre.

    d) The council should make some
        improvements to the bus shelter.

Putting Things in the Right Order

Think about what order you say things in

1) Write your points in a **sensible order**.

2) This will make it easier for the reader to **understand** what you're saying.

Group similar information together

1) Write **everything** about **one point** first, and then move on to the **next point**.

2) **Don't** go back to writing about the first point again.

EXAMPLE:

> 1) You are running a race to raise money for charity.
>   Write an email to your friend to tell them about it.

> I am running a marathon to raise money for charity. I am hoping to raise about £600. I have asked everyone I know to sponsor me. I have been training for five months. I go for a run before work every day, and I go to the gym twice a week.

Here, the text talks about raising money for charity.

Here, the text is about the training for the marathon. There is no information about raising money.

Write your most important point first

This tells the reader what you are writing about **straight away**.

Car for sale. I'm selling my Blue Ford Mondeo for £2500.

The most important point is that a car is for sale.

You are all invited to dinner at my house on Saturday. Come any time after 8 pm.

The most important point is the invitation to dinner.

Practice Questions

In each question there is a writing task and three points to include in the answer.
Write out the points, putting them in the **best order**.

1) Write a personal statement to apply for a carpentry course.

   - Say how the course would be helpful for your future
   - Talk about the skills and experience you have
   - Say that you want to apply for the course

   a) ....

   b) ....

   c) ....

2) You are making cakes for a cake stall. Write an email to a friend asking them to help.

   - Ask them to bake some cakes
   - Tell them when the cakes should be ready by
   - Tell them about the cake stall

   a) ....

   b) ....

   c) ....

3) Write a letter to the town hall asking to use a room for your first aid course.

   - Say how the course would be good for the community
   - Say you would like to use the room for your course
   - Give details of when you would like to use the room

   a) ....

   b) ....

   c) ....

Using Paragraphs

A paragraph is a group of sentences

1) These sentences talk about the **same thing** or **follow on** from each other.

2) Start a new paragraph on a **new line**.

> with no respect for anyone else living in the street.
>
> I have tried to speak to them many times, but it has not worked. They don't listen to me, and get angry. ← *This is the end of one paragraph.*
>
> We really cannot carry on like this. I do not want to be forced out of my own home. Please can you visit them, and make it clear that they need to

This is the start of a new paragraph. Leave a space at the beginning of the first line. You could leave a line blank instead.

Paragraphs make your writing clearer

1) Give each **point** its own **paragraph**.

2) Your **first** paragraph should say **what** your answer is **about**.

3) The **middle** paragraphs should add more **details**.

4) Your **last** paragraph should **sum up** your main point.

Start a new paragraph when something changes

Start a new paragraph when you talk about a different **thing**, **person**, **place** or **time**.

This sentence is about a different thing, so it is in a new paragraph.

> I am friendly and enjoy working with other people. This would be useful for working in your salon.
>
> I studied hairdressing at college and have learnt how to style different types of hair.
>
> I worked in a beauty salon after college. This has taught me

This sentence is about a different time, so it is in a new paragraph.

Practice Question

1) Read this piece of writing about winter celebrations.
   Rewrite it underneath, dividing it into **three** paragraphs.

> People all over the world celebrate the start of the new year. They count the seconds until midnight on the 31st of December, to mark the start of a new calendar year. Hogmanay is a Scottish celebration which is also held on the 31st of December. Some people carry on the celebrations until the 2nd of January, which is also a bank holiday in Scotland. Chinese New Year falls on a different date each year, and is celebrated in at least nine countries. The festivities last for around two weeks.

....

....

....

....

....

....

....

....

....

....

....

....

....

Using Headings and Bullet Points

Headings and subheadings help organise your writing

1) **Headings** and **subheadings** divide a text up into **sections**.

2) They are usually in a **bigger font**, **underlined** or **bold**.

3) They are often used in **newspaper articles**, **instructions** and **leaflets**.

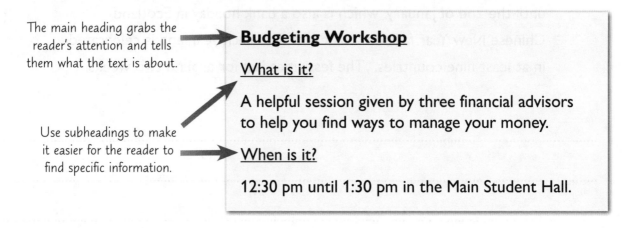

The main heading grabs the reader's attention and tells them what the text is about.

Use subheadings to make it easier for the reader to find specific information.

Budgeting Workshop

What is it?

A helpful session given by three financial advisors to help you find ways to manage your money.

When is it?

12:30 pm until 1:30 pm in the Main Student Hall.

Bullet points are used for lists

1) Use bullet points to make **lists** of information **easier to read**.

2) They are often used in **instructions, leaflets** and **advertisements**.

3) **Numbered lists** can be used instead of bullet points. This is usually for things that are in a particular **order**.

NANA'S VANILLA SPONGE CAKE

Ingredients:

- 200 g caster sugar
- 200 g self-raising flour
- 200 g butter
- 4 eggs
- 2 tbsp milk
- vanilla extract

Bullet points separate the list of ingredients into short, clear bits of text.

Method:

1) Preheat the oven to 190 °C.
2) Beat the butter and sugar in a bowl until creamy.
3) Slowly beat in the eggs, one by one.

The instructions are laid out as a numbered list so that each step is done in the correct order.

1) Read this piece of writing about a gardening business.

> Hello, my name is Grace and I have a gardening business. I have been a gardener for 12 years and have recently become self-employed. I offer lawn mowing, hedge cutting, general garden maintenance and planting services. I can also offer landscaping evaluations. Prices will vary depending on the difficulty of the job, but please contact me for a rough quote. To contact me, please email: gardeningwithgrace@azmail.co.uk.

Complete the poster below by adding a heading, subheadings and bullet points. Use the writing above to help you. The first subheading and bullet point has been done for you.

Hello, my name is Grace and I have a gardening business. I have been a gardener for 12 years and have recently become self-employed.

My services

I am happy to help with the following jobs:

- Lawn mowing
-
-
-
-

My prices vary depending on the difficulty of the job,
but please contact me for a rough quote.

To get in touch, please email: gardeningwithgrace@azmail.co.uk

---

Writing Letters

Letters have a greeting at the top and a sign-off at the bottom

1) For someone you **don't know**:

   - Use a greeting like '**Dear Mr Jones**' if you know their name.

   - If you don't know their name, write '**Dear Sir or Madam**'.

   - End with '**Yours sincerely**' if you know their name or '**Yours faithfully**' if you don't.

2) For somebody you **know well**:

   - Use a greeting like '**Dear Sarah**' or '**Hi Mark**'.

   - End with '**Best wishes**' or '**See you soon**'.

Follow the rules for writing letters

1) Use **serious language** in letters to someone **important** or someone you **don't know**.

2) You should be **polite** to create a good impression.

3) If you are writing to a **friend** or **family member**, you can use **chatty** language.

4) Write your letter in **paragraphs**.

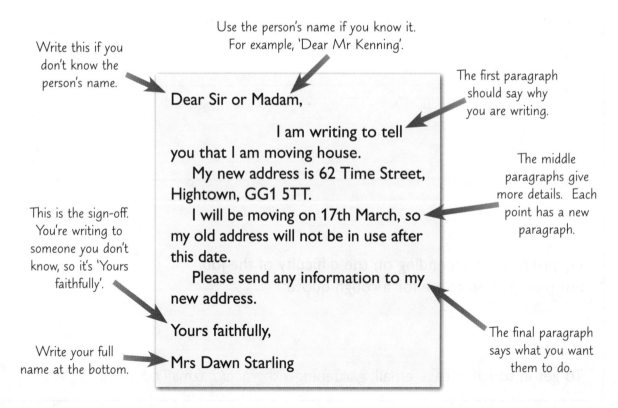

Write this if you don't know the person's name.

Use the person's name if you know it. For example, 'Dear Mr Kenning'.

The first paragraph should say why you are writing.

Dear Sir or Madam,

    I am writing to tell you that I am moving house.
    My new address is 62 Time Street, Hightown, GG1 5TT.
    I will be moving on 17th March, so my old address will not be in use after this date.
    Please send any information to my new address.

Yours faithfully,

Mrs Dawn Starling

The middle paragraphs give more details. Each point has a new paragraph.

This is the sign-off. You're writing to someone you don't know, so it's 'Yours faithfully'.

Write your full name at the bottom.

The final paragraph says what you want them to do.

Practice Question

1) A bus company is planning to introduce a new bus service in your area.
You use the bus regularly, so extra services would be useful for you.

Write a letter to the company to tell them what you think about the new bus service.

You should include:

- Why you think the new bus service is a good idea
- When you think the new buses should run
- Who you think would use them.

Dear _____ ,

....

....

....

....

....

....

....

....

....

....

....

....

....

Writing Emails

Emails also start with a greeting and end with a sign-off

1) If you **know** the person, use a **greeting** like '**Dear Dad**' or '**Hi Hanif**'.

2) If you **don't** know them, write something like '**Dear Mr Ogden**', or '**Dear Sir or Madam**' if you don't know their name.

3) If you **know** the person well, use a **sign-off** like '**See you soon**' or '**Best wishes**'.

4) If you **don't** know them, write something like '**Many thanks**' or '**Best regards**'.

Use paragraphs in your email

1) Your **first** paragraph should say **why** you are writing the email.

2) Write a new **paragraph** for **each** point you want to make.

3) Your **last** paragraph should say what you would like the person to **do**.

Lay out emails correctly

Fill in the boxes that you are given.

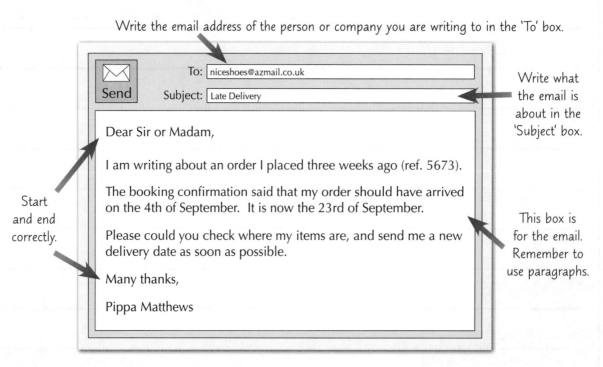

Write the email address of the person or company you are writing to in the 'To' box.

To: niceshoes@azmail.co.uk

Subject: Late Delivery

Write what the email is about in the 'Subject' box.

Start and end correctly.

Dear Sir or Madam,

I am writing about an order I placed three weeks ago (ref. 5673).

The booking confirmation said that my order should have arrived on the 4th of September. It is now the 23rd of September.

Please could you check where my items are, and send me a new delivery date as soon as possible.

Many thanks,

Pippa Matthews

This box is for the email. Remember to use paragraphs.

Practice Question

1) Read this email from a work friend about changes to the canteen menu.

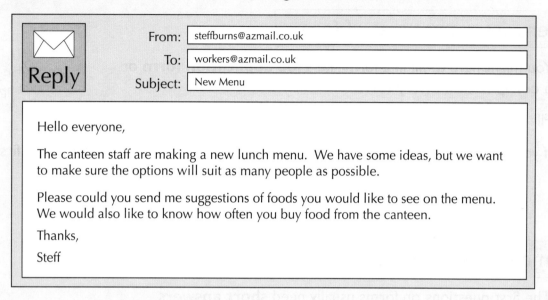

From:	steffburns@azmail.co.uk
To:	workers@azmail.co.uk
Subject:	New Menu

Hello everyone,

The canteen staff are making a new lunch menu. We have some ideas, but we want to make sure the options will suit as many people as possible.

Please could you send me suggestions of foods you would like to see on the menu. We would also like to know how often you buy food from the canteen.

Thanks,

Steff

Write a short reply which says:

• What you would like to see on the new menu
• How often you buy food from the canteen.

| To: | |
| Subject: | |

....

....

....

....

....

....

....

....

....

Filling in Forms

There are many types of form

1) You might have to fill in a form like a **job application form** or a **competition entry form**.

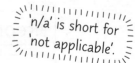

'n/a' is short for 'not applicable'.

2) Fill in **every part** of the form. Write '**n/a**' if something doesn't apply to you.

3) If you are asked about your **education** or **jobs**, start with the **most recent** first.

Some answers will be very short

1) The first questions on forms usually need **short answers**.

> Name: _____   Date of Birth: _____
>
> Address: _____
>
> _____

2) You do not need to write in **full sentences** for **short** answers.

Some answers will be longer

1) For example, 'Why do you think you would be good at this job?'

2) You will have a much **bigger space** to write in.

Explain what happened:

You will need to write a few paragraphs for longer answers.

3) You need to write in **full sentences**.

Practice Question

1) You want to apply to be a customer service assistant at a call centre.
   The company is looking for people who are fast learners and who
   have basic computer skills and good communication skills.

   Fill in the application form below.
   You can make up realistic details if you need to.

   You should include:

   • Why you would like the job
   • Any work experience you have
   • Any other useful skills you have.

Happy Chatting Call Centres

Name: _____   Date of birth: _____

Position applied for: _____

Why are you right for this job?

....

....

....

....

....

....

....

....

....

....

Writing Instructions

Instructions are written in the order they will be done

1) Instructions are often written as **numbered points** or **bullet points**.

2) They should always be written in the **order** they need to be done.

See p.12 and p.38 for more on bullet points.

These instructions are written as numbered points.

Setting up your new phone

1. Charge the phone fully.
2. Turn the phone on.
3. Enter your email address.
4. Set up a new passcode.

These instructions would be impossible to follow if they were in the wrong order.

Instructions need to be clear

1) **Simple language** makes instructions **easy** to understand.

2) There is not much **description**. This makes the points **clearer**.

Directions from the church to the wedding reception

• Turn left at the end of Church Street.
• Continue until the roundabout.
• Take the first exit onto George Street.
• When you get to the primary school, turn right.
• The Fairfield Hotel will be on your left.

Instructions are usually broken up into short sentences.

If the fire alarm sounds:

• Leave the building quickly and calmly.
• Do not go back for your belongings.
• Meet at the carpark.

These instructions don't give any details that are not needed.

Practice Question

1) The paragraphs below tell you how to put up a shelf.

<u>Putting up a shelf</u>

Decide where you want your shelf to be, and mark the position of the brackets on the wall with a pencil. Use a spirit level to make sure that the brackets will be level. Then, drill some holes into the wall ready for the screws to fit into.

Using a screwdriver, screw the brackets to the wall, making sure that the screws are fairly tight. Attach the shelf to the brackets with more screws, making sure that they will not move when the shelf is being used.

Rewrite the paragraphs as instructions. Make each instruction as simple as possible. Use bullet points to make your instructions clearer.

....

....

....

....

....

....

....

....

....

....

....

....

....

Writing Reports

Reports are pieces of factual writing

1) This means that they contain lots of **information**.

2) For example, an **accident report**, a **personal statement** for a job or a **newspaper article**.

3) You are usually writing to someone you **don't know**, so your writing should not be chatty.

> A personal statement is a piece of writing about yourself and your skills. They are usually written to apply for a job or a college course.

Organise your ideas before writing your report

Think about **why** you are writing the report, and write notes about the **important facts**.

EXAMPLE:

1) You left your purse on the bus. Write down some information for the bus company telling them what happened and what your purse is like.

You need to tell the bus company about your lost purse.

- Bus 6B Monday 6th October, 10.30 am.
- Yellow purse.
- Cards inside.
- Contact me if you find it.

You should include facts like the date and time you lost your purse and what it looks like.

Write your report using your notes

1) Start a new **paragraph** for each new **point**.

2) You might want to **divide** your report into **sections**.

Separating the information into sections makes it easier to read.

Incident
I left my purse on bus 6B on Monday 6th October. The bus left the station at 10.30 am. I left it on a seat near the front of the bus.

Description
It's a yellow leather purse. There are cards and my driving licence inside. There is a photo of my daughter in the side pocket.

Practice Question

1) You organised a charity fundraising day at work. You receive this email from a work friend:

Reply	From: <u>Mike Simpson</u>
	Subject: Fundraising day report

Hello,

Your fundraising day was brilliant. I hope you raised lots of money.

Could you write a short report about the day for the company newsletter?

You could include a bit about the day itself, how much money you raised and what the hospital will spend the money on.

Thank you,
Mike

Write a report about the fundraising day using the suggestions in the email.
Divide your writing into sections to make it clearer.

....

....

....

....

....

....

....

....

....

....

....

....

Making Sentences

Always write in sentences

1) You get marks for using **full sentences** in the writing test.

2) You **don't** have to use full sentences in a **plan**. You can use notes or bullet points instead.

3) If you have to write a **draft**, you should use **full sentences**.

A sentence must make sense on its own

1) Every sentence needs an **action word**. This is called a **verb**.

Every morning my neighbour runs to work.

This is the verb. It tells you what happens.

2) A sentence needs **someone** or **something** to 'do' the verb.

The machine is 'doing' the action.

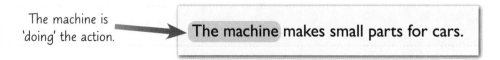

The machine makes small parts for cars.

3) Some sentences tell you **who** or **what** the action is being **done to**.

I sold my coin collection yesterday.

The selling was 'done' to the coin collection.

Make sentences by putting all the parts together

Put the person or thing **doing** the action and the **verb** together.

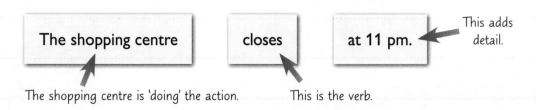

The shopping centre   closes   at 11 pm.

This adds detail.

The shopping centre is 'doing' the action.   This is the verb.

Practice Questions

1) Underline the verb in each sentence.

   a)   Our manager writes the timetable.

   b)   My neighbour organised a party.

   c)   I applied for the job today.

   d)   We eat our lunch in the canteen.

   e)   At college I studied engineering.

2) Underline who or what is doing the action in each sentence.

   a)   The car broke down on the way to work.

   b)   Our cat caught a mouse.

   c)   You cycled to work last week.

   d)   I read the application form.

   e)   My sister works in a bank.

3) Read these notes giving details of a computing course. Rewrite the notes in full sentences.

> Starts 9 am, ends 5 pm
> Lunch break 1 pm
> Two coffee breaks
> Bring pen and notebook.

....

....

....

....

....

....

Using Joining Words

Use joining words to make your writing sound better

Joining words **connect** two sentences together to make **one long sentence**.

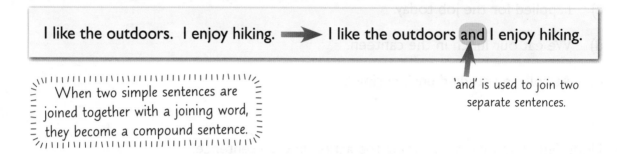

I like the outdoors. I enjoy hiking. ➡ I like the outdoors **and** I enjoy hiking.

'and' is used to join two separate sentences.

When two simple sentences are joined together with a joining word, they become a compound sentence.

'But' and 'or' disagree with a point

1) Use '**but**' to **disagree** with something that's just been said.

Marcus usually works the late shift, **but** he is in early today.

2) Use '**or**' to give **another option**.

We could go clubbing tonight, **or** we could go bowling.

'Because' and 'so' add more detail

Use '**because**' and '**so**' to **explain** things.

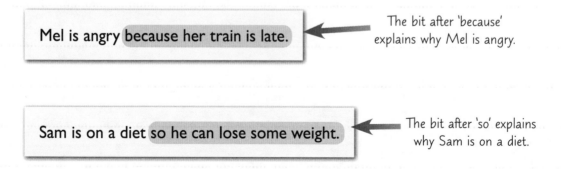

Mel is angry **because her train is late**.

The bit after 'because' explains why Mel is angry.

Sam is on a diet **so he can lose some weight**.

The bit after 'so' explains why Sam is on a diet.

Practice Questions

1) Choose 'and', 'or', 'so', 'because' or 'but' to complete these sentences.

   a)   The college offers childcare courses, ... it organises work placements.

   b)   She was late for work .... her alarm did not go off.

   c)   I want to buy a bike .... I can get fit.

   d)   They went to the shop, ... it had already closed.

   e)   You should try this tea .... it is lovely.

   f)   I will either borrow the blue shoes, ... buy the pink shoes.

   g)   He built the cupboard carefully, ... it was still a bit wobbly.

   h)   At the park, we saw Ryan, ... he had his new dog with him.

   i)   Bridget didn't know if she should go for a run, ... go swimming.

2) Finish these sentences, adding an explanation.

   a)   I cannot come to work today because ....

   b)   I am going to buy a car so ....

   c)   She painted her room because ....

   d)   Do not go in the kitchen because ....

   e)   I woke up early so ....

   f)   I took the curtains back to the shop because ....

   g)   My brother is visiting me so ....

   h)   He brought his wallet so ....

'A', 'An' and 'The'

These three words give you more information about nouns

1) **'A'**, **'an'** or **'the'** can go before nouns.

2) They tell the reader if something is **general** or **specific**.

3) Make sure you use 'a', 'an' and 'the' correctly in your writing.

'A' and 'an' are used for general things

'A' and **'an'** show you that a noun refers to **an example** of something, not a **specific** thing.

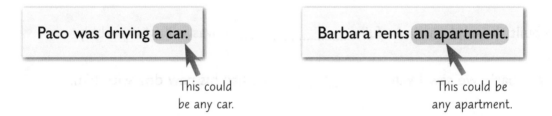

Paco was driving a car.
This could be any car.

Barbara rents an apartment.
This could be any apartment.

You use 'an' and 'a' with different words

1) Use **'an'** when the **next word** starts with a **vowel sound** — e.g. 'an apple' or 'an orange'.

2) Use **'a'** when the **next word** starts with a **consonant sound** — e.g. 'a banana' or 'a lime'.

3) Be careful — some words are **spelt** with one letter but **sound** like another.

4) For example, 'universe' sounds like 'you-niverse', so you use **'a'** instead of **'an'**.

'The' is used for specific things

'The' shows you that a noun refers to one **specific** thing.

Clara was driving the green car.
This means a particular car.

Zaid rents the large apartment.
This means a particular apartment.

Practice Questions

1) Are the underlined parts of each sentence below specific or general? Circle your answer.

   a)   <u>The job</u> was advertised online.   specific / general

   b)   Keith built <u>a bookcase</u> by himself.   specific / general

   c)   I bought a pie from <u>the bakery</u>.   specific / general

   d)   <u>An ant</u> crawled up the wall.   specific / general

   e)   It was very cold in <u>the igloo</u>.   specific / general

2) Circle the correct option to complete each sentence below.

   a)   He couldn't believe **a / an** ticket could cost that much.

   b)   There was **a / an** unusual feeling in the office today.

   c)   Gill climbed **a / an** tall tree in the middle of the forest.

   d)   You are **a / an** inspiration to so many young people.

   e)   I ordered **a / an** hamburger and a drink.

   f)   I'm looking for **a / an** orange sofa.

3) Choose 'a', 'an' or 'the' to complete these sentences.

   a)   .... spider in my room is huge.

   b)   There was .... unusual smell in the kitchen.

   c)   She couldn't see because .... sun was in her eyes.

   d)   .... Managing Director of the company came to my party.

   e)   When I was in Japan, there was .... big earthquake.

   f)   They wished they'd gone to .... different hotel.

   g)   Leslie decided he was going to buy a puppy at .... weekend.

Writing About Different Times

A verb is a 'doing' or 'being' word

Use verbs to describe what something **does** or **is**.

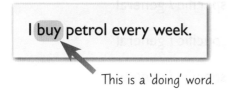
I **buy** petrol every week.

This is a 'doing' word.

Jack **is** the Safety Officer.

This is a 'being' word.

Use the present tense to say what is happening now

Most verbs in the **present tense** follow the same **verb pattern**:

If you are writing about 'I', 'you', 'we' or 'they', you don't need to change the verb.

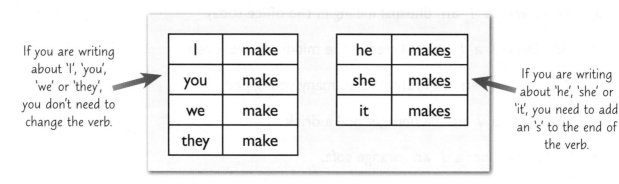

I	make
you	make
we	make
they	make

he	make**s**
she	make**s**
it	make**s**

If you are writing about 'he', 'she' or 'it', you need to add an 's' to the end of the verb.

How you change the verb depends on who is doing it

Use the **verb pattern** to work out the correct ending.

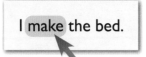
I **make** the bed.

The verb pattern shows that you don't need to change the verb when you are writing about 'I'.

She **makes** cupcakes.

You need to add an 's' to the verb because you are talking about 'she'.

They **sell** bicycles.

You don't need to change the verb when you are writing about 'they'.

It **sells** furniture.

You need to add an 's' to the verb because you are talking about 'it'.

Writing About Different Times

Use the past tense to say what has already happened

1) For most verbs, you need to add '**ed**' to the end to make them past tense.

walk ➡ I walked

touch ➡ You touched

2) If the verb already ends in '**e**', just add a '**d**' to the end.

hope ➡ They hoped

invite ➡ We invited

Not all past tense verbs add 'ed'

1) Some verbs follow their own **patterns**.

You need to learn these verbs.

Verb	Past Tense
I do	I did
I have	I had
I see	I saw
I get	I got
I take	I took

Verb	Past Tense
I am / we are	I was / we were
I go	I went
I make	I made
I come	I came
I think	I thought

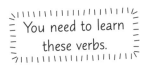

Use 'was' for 'I', 'he', 'she' and 'it'. Use 'were' for 'you', 'we' and 'they'.

These are just a few examples. There are other verbs that act differently too.

2) Some verbs **don't change** at all in the past tense.

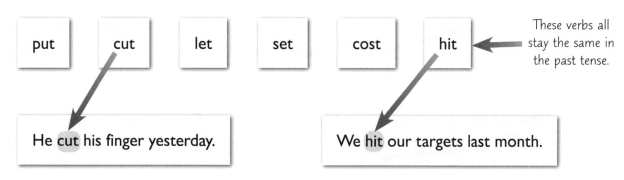

put   cut   let   set   cost   hit

These verbs all stay the same in the past tense.

He cut his finger yesterday.

We hit our targets last month.

Writing About Different Times

To talk about the future you can use 'I am going'...

1) Talk about future actions by using the correct version of **'I am going'**.

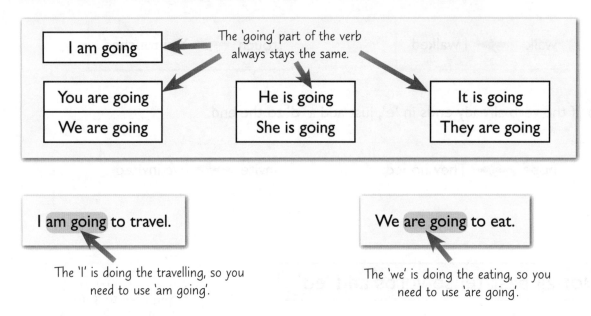

| I am going |
| You are going |
| We are going |

The 'going' part of the verb always stays the same.

| He is going |
| She is going |

| It is going |
| They are going |

I **am going** to travel.

The 'I' is doing the travelling, so you need to use 'am going'.

We **are going** to eat.

The 'we' is doing the eating, so you need to use 'are going'.

2) You need to put the word **'to' in front** of the action being done.

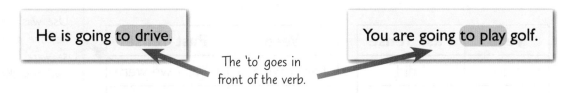

He is going **to drive.**

You are going **to play** golf.

The 'to' goes in front of the verb.

...or you can use 'will'

1) You can also use **'will'** to talk about things in the future.

2) The 'will' part **never changes**. It doesn't matter **who** is doing the action.

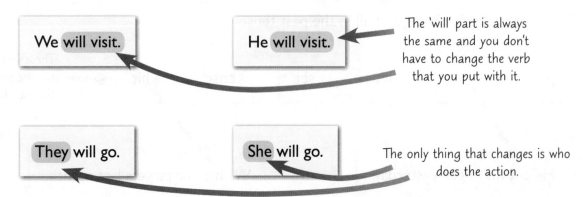

We **will visit.**

He **will visit.**

The 'will' part is always the same and you don't have to change the verb that you put with it.

They **will go.**

She **will go.**

The only thing that changes is who does the action.

Practice Questions

1) Each sentence is about the past, present or future. Circle the correct time for each one.

   a) I went to the cinema.   past   present   future

   b) The sign says 'Stop'.   past   present   future

   c) You are going to go on holiday.   past   present   future

   d) They catch the bus to work.   past   present   future

   e) We will take photos to show you.   past   present   future

2) Circle the correct verb to complete each sentence.

   a) Simon **cooks** / **cooked** pasta for dinner last night.

   b) Ayana **write** / **writes** the article.

   c) I **washed** / **wash** the car this morning.

   d) The trees **was** / **were** blowing in the wind.

   e) You **is** / **are** organised today.

3) Rewrite these sentences so they make sense.

   a) I buy four tomatoes but they were rotten.

   ....

   b) We was at football yesterday.

   ....

   c) I will catch the train, but I was still late.

   ....

   d) You is going to go to the beach tomorrow.

   ....

   e) They go to a meeting yesterday.

   ....

Common Mistakes with Verbs

The verb must match the person doing the action

Check **how many people** are doing the action to work out if the **verb** should **change**.

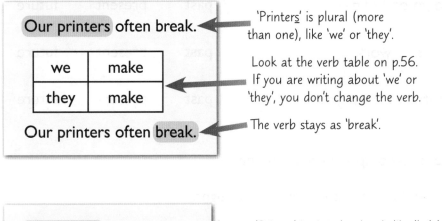

Our printers often break.

we	make
they	make

Our printers often break.

'Printers' is plural (more than one), like 'we' or 'they'.

Look at the verb table on p.56. If you are writing about 'we' or 'they', you don't change the verb.

The verb stays as 'break'.

Our printer often break.

it	makes

Our printer often breaks.

'Printer' is singular (one), like 'he', 'she' or 'it'.

If you are writing about an 'it', you need to add an 's' to the verb.

The verb becomes 'breaks'.

Use the right 'being' word to go with the person

1) Use '**is**' when you are talking about **one person** or **thing**.

2) Use '**are**' when you are talking about **more than one person** or **thing**.

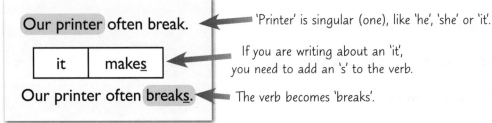

There is one security guard.

There are two security guards.

There is one security guard, so use 'is'.

There are two security guards, so use 'are'.

'Been' and 'done' always go with 'have' or 'has'

Always use '**have**' or '**has**' when you write 'been' or 'done'.

I have done the report you asked for.

You can't miss out the 'have' part. 'I done' doesn't make sense.

Common Mistakes with Verbs

Don't confuse 'could've' and 'could of'

1) Always write '**could have**'. Never write 'could of' because it doesn't mean anything.

2) It's the same for '**might have**' and '**should have**'.

> He could have cleaned the house. I should have told him to.

It's always 'could have'. You can't say 'could of' or 'could has'.

Practice Questions

1) The verb in each of these sentences is wrong. Rewrite the sentence with the correct verb.

   a) The children plays in the park.

   ....

   b) The fire alarm ring on Tuesdays.

   ....

   c) She walk to the shops every day.

   ....

   d) I throws away the bananas.

   ....

2) Rewrite each sentence so that it makes sense.

   a) I could of done it yesterday, but I forgot.

   ....

   b) You should of come to the party.

   ....

   c) They done the shopping already.

   ....

Punctuating Sentences

Sentences start with capital letters

Every sentence should begin with a **capital letter**.

> Men were working on the road. That is why I was late for work.

Names also start with capital letters

1) Names of **people** and **places** begin with capital letters.

> Fiona is going to America soon.

2) The **days** of the week and **months** of the year also start with capital letters.

> Next Tuesday is the last day in January.

3) '**I**' is **always** a capital letter when you are talking about yourself.

4) **Don't** use capital letters in the **middle** of a word.

Sentences end with full stops

1) Use a **full stop** to show that your sentence has **finished**.

> The car kept rattling. He pulled over.

You need a full stop and a capital letter every time you finish one sentence and start another.

2) You can use an **exclamation mark** if you're saying something really **amazing**.

> I can't believe the exhaust has fallen off!

This exclamation mark shows shock and surprise.

3) Try not to use **too many** exclamation marks, or they lose their effect.

Punctuating Sentences

Questions end with question marks

1) A question should **start** with a **capital letter**.

2) It should end with a **question mark** instead of a full stop.

Are you tired? ← Use a question mark here.
You don't need a full stop as well.

Practice Question

1) Use capital letters, full stops, exclamation marks and question marks to write these sentences correctly.

a) somebody stop that bus

....

b) my manager said i could take the day off

....

c) who should i write a letter to

....

d) look how bright the sun is today

....

e) would you like to join our tennis club

....

f) we want to go to cornwall for our holiday

....

g) does this train go directly from portsmouth to york

....

h) i am going to the cinema with anita tonight

....

Using Commas

Commas separate things in a list

1) **Commas** can **break up lists** of **three** or **more** things.

2) Put a **comma** after **each thing** in the list.

3) Between the **last two things** you **don't** need a **comma**. Use '**and**' or '**or**' instead.

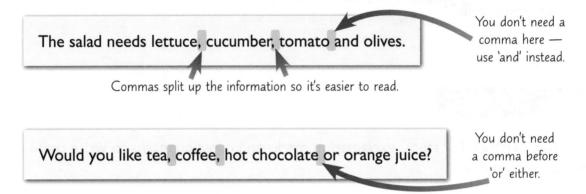

The salad needs lettuce, cucumber, tomato and olives.

You don't need a comma here — use 'and' instead.

Commas split up the information so it's easier to read.

Would you like tea, coffee, hot chocolate or orange juice?

You don't need a comma before 'or' either.

Commas can join two points

1) **Two sentences** can be **joined** using a **joining word** and a **comma**.

2) **Joining words** are words like '**and**', '**but**' and '**so**'.

3) The comma is added **before** the joining word.

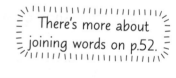

There's more about joining words on p.52.

The road is closed. I'll take the train. ⟶ The road is closed, **so** I'll take the train.

I have to clean. I can't find my mop. ⟶ I have to clean, **but** I can't find my mop.

I have a son. He is really energetic. ⟶ I have a son, **and** he is really energetic.

Don't use too many commas in the same sentence. Shorter sentences separated with full stops are easier to understand.

1) Correct these sentences by putting commas in the right places.

   a) It would be nice to visit Paris Rome or Madrid.

   b) He has a week off work so he's going to relax.

   c) I'm going shopping today and I'm going swimming tomorrow.

   d) The dish needs three potatoes one onion two peppers and four eggs.

   e) They had planned to go hiking but it was raining.

   f) Jasmine Elijah and Alex are too ill to come to work today.

   g) They had strawberries apples pears and mangoes for sale.

   h) The cinema was closed so we went to the park.

   i) Employees should be punctual reliable and hard-working.

   j) Lisa is getting married and Tonya is her bridesmaid.

   k) They were going to go on holiday but their flight was cancelled.

   l) We saw penguins sea lions and elephants at the zoo.

2) Join the following sentences together using a comma followed by 'and', 'but' or 'so'.

   a) It was a beautiful day. Ollie went to the beach.

   ....

   b) Jade's car broke down. The bus was cancelled.

   ....

   c) Liam wanted to get tickets. They were sold out.

   ....

   d) Emily's phone was stolen. She called the police.

   ....

   e) The weather forecast predicted rain. It's sunny.

   ....

Alphabetical Order

You could be asked to put words in alphabetical order

1) You might have a question where you have to write words in **alphabetical order**.

2) This is easier if the **first letters** are **different**.

EXAMPLE:

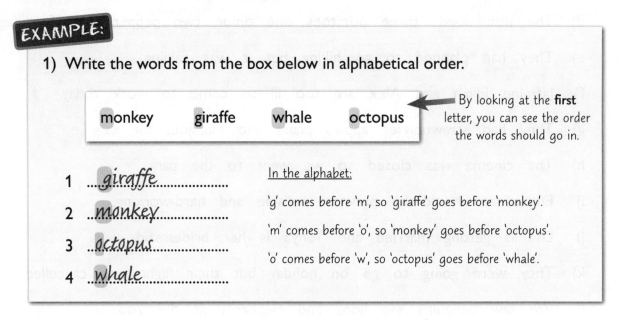

1) Write the words from the box below in alphabetical order.

| monkey | giraffe | whale | octopus |

By looking at the **first** letter, you can see the order the words should go in.

1 _giraffe_
2 _monkey_
3 _octopus_
4 _whale_

In the alphabet:

'g' comes before 'm', so 'giraffe' goes before 'monkey'.

'm' comes before 'o', so 'monkey' goes before 'octopus'.

'o' comes before 'w', so 'octopus' goes before 'whale'.

3) Ordering the words gets trickier if they **all start** with the **same letter**.

4) If the **first letters** are the **same**, then order them by their **second** letters.

5) If the **first and second** letters are the same, then order them by their **third** letters.

EXAMPLE:

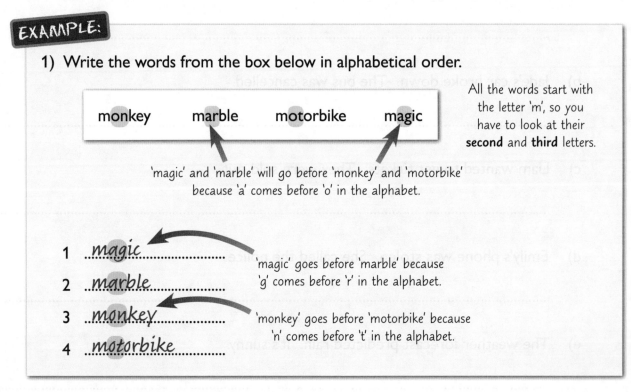

1) Write the words from the box below in alphabetical order.

| monkey | marble | motorbike | magic |

All the words start with the letter 'm', so you have to look at their **second** and **third** letters.

'magic' and 'marble' will go before 'monkey' and 'motorbike' because 'a' comes before 'o' in the alphabet.

1 _magic_
2 _marble_
3 _monkey_
4 _motorbike_

'magic' goes before 'marble' because 'g' comes before 'r' in the alphabet.

'monkey' goes before 'motorbike' because 'n' comes before 't' in the alphabet.

Practice Questions

1) Put the following words in alphabetical order.

a) Samantha   Geoffrey   Richard   Abigail

....

b) books   radio   television   picture

....

c) obsession   badger   across   popular

....

d) network   nugget   native   nought

....

e) mountain   market   million   merchant

....

f) fiction   familiar   frequent   formal

....

g) settlement   secure   separate   serve

....

h) jealous   jester   jewel   jersey

....

i) carnival   canopy   cabbage   category

....

j) trumpet   terrace   telephone   transport

....

k) official   opening   opportunity   occupy

....

l) desert   danger   double   dolphin

....

Making Plurals

Plural means 'more than one'

1) To make most words **plural**, you put an '**s**' on the **end**.

one car ➡ two cars

The 's' means that there is more than one car.

2) If a word **ends** with '**ch**', '**x**', '**s**', '**sh**' or '**z**', put '**es**' on the **end** to make it plural.

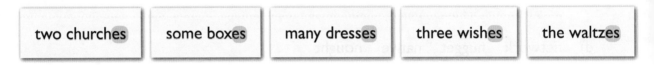

| two churches | some boxes | many dresses | three wishes | the waltzes |

Words ending with 'y' have different rules

1) Some words end with a **vowel** ('a', 'e', 'i', 'o' or 'u') and then a '**y**'.

2) To make these words **plural**, put an '**s**' on the end.

| two days | his keys | five guys |

All these words end in a vowel and a 'y', so they just need an 's'.

3) Some words end with a **consonant** (any letter that isn't a **vowel**) and then a '**y**'.

4) To make them **plural**, change the '**y**' to '**ies**'.

fly ➡ flies   city ➡ cities

Words ending with 'f' or 'fe' need a 'v'

1) To make words ending with '**f**' or '**fe**' **plural** you need a '**v**'.

2) Take off the '**f**' or '**fe**' from the end of the word and add '**ves**' instead.

one shelf ➡ two shelves   a thief ➡ three thieves

Making Plurals

Some words don't follow a pattern

1) To make some words plural, you have to change the **spelling** of the word.

tooth ➡ teeth   woman ➡ women   mouse ➡ mice

2) Some words **don't change at all**.

fish   deer   sheep

You would always say 'two sheep', never 'two sheeps'.

Practice Questions

1) Write the plural of each word.

a) plant ....

d) half ....

b) boy ....

e) country ....

c) sandwich ....

f) foot ....

2) Each sentence has an incorrect plural. Rewrite the sentences with the correct plural.

a) The loafs of bread I bought were too hard.

....

b) Can childs eat at your restaurant?

....

c) There are lots of gooses by the lake today.

....

d) I talked about my hobbys in the interview.

....

Adding Prefixes

Prefixes are used to make new words

Prefixes are **letters** that are added to the **start** of words.

un + lock ➝ unlock

re + appear ➝ reappear

Prefixes change the meaning of a word

When you add a **prefix**, it changes the **meaning** of the word.

un + lucky ➝ unlucky

dis + obey ➝ disobey

Prefixes can be tricky

1) There are a few prefixes that make a word mean the **opposite**.

2) For example, **'un'**, **'in'**, **'im'**, and **'dis'**. It's easy to get confused between them.

unpopular   indefinite   impolite   disorganised ⬅ Learn how to spell these words with prefixes.

Adding a prefix won't change the spelling

Adding a **prefix doesn't** change the spelling of a word.

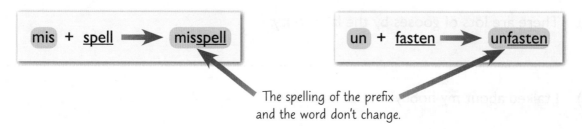

mis + spell ➝ misspell

un + fasten ➝ unfasten

The spelling of the prefix and the word don't change.

Adding Prefixes

Some prefixes need a hyphen before the word

1) **Hyphens** can be used to join a **prefix** to a **root word**.

2) You often need a hyphen when the prefix **ends** in the same letter that the root word **begins with**.

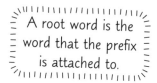

A root word is the word that the prefix is attached to.

re + enter → re-enter

co + operate → co-operate

The hyphen goes between the prefix and the vowel.

Practice Questions

1) Rewrite each word so it is spelt correctly.

   a) dissagree ....

   c) missmatch ....

   b) unnpack ....

   d) innformal ....

2) Each sentence below has a mistake. Rewrite the sentences with the mistake fixed.

   a) She is the coowner of the company.

   ....

   b) The instructions were unecessary.

   ....

   c) She needs to reevaluate her choices.

   ....

   d) He wished he could be imortal.

   ....

   e) The two brothers were not disimilar.

   ....

   f) She misttrusted every word that he said.

   ....

Adding Suffixes

Suffixes are used to make new words

Suffixes are letters that are added to the **end** of words.

love + ly ➡ lovely

hope + ful ➡ hopeful

Suffixes change the meaning of a word

When you add a **suffix**, it changes the **meaning** of the word.

climb + er ➡ climber ⬅ Adding the suffix '-er' turns the verb into a noun.

Suffixes can be tricky

1) Some **suffixes** can be hard to spell.

2) **'ful'** is a common suffix. Words ending in 'ful' are always spelt with **one 'l'** at the end.

successful   helpful   beautiful   useful

Adding a suffix might change the spelling

1) If you add a **suffix** to a word, sometimes the spelling **changes**.

2) If a word ends in an 'e' and the **first letter** of the suffix is a **vowel**, you **drop** the 'e'.

love + ing ➡ loving

care + er ➡ carer

3) If a word ends with a **consonant** and then a 'y', change the 'y' to an 'i'.

dry + ed ➡ dried

happy + ness ➡ happiness

Practice Questions

1) Add the suffix to the word to correctly spell a new word.

   a) certain + ly   ....

   b) purpose + ful   ....

   c) use + er   ....

   d) supply + ed   ....

   e) lonely + ness   ....

   f) make + ing   ....

2) Circle the correct word to complete these sentences.

   a) A **developer / developper** is inspecting the house today.

   b) The king was a very **merciful / mercyful** ruler.

   c) The stale sponge cake was **crumblly / crumbly** and dry.

   d) She **tried / tryed** to phone the call centre again.

   e) His **lazyness / laziness** isn't very professional.

3) Each sentence below has a mistake. Rewrite the sentences with the mistake fixed.

   a) I remembered the file as I was leaveing.

   ....

   b) The weather was particularlly wet today.

   ....

   c) She was doubtfull that he would attend the party.

   ....

   d) I'm afraid you are not qualifyed for this job.

   ....

Common Word Sounds

The 'sh' and 'ch' sounds are quite similar

1) The letter **'s'** is most commonly used to spell the **'sh' sound**.

shampoo — The 'sh' makes the sound here.

sugar — The 's' makes the sound here.

session — The 'ss' makes the sound here.

2) But **'ci'** and **'ti'** can also spell the **'sh' sound** when they're followed by a vowel.

especially   delicious   condition   patient

3) The letters **'ch'** can spell both the **'sh' sound** and the **'ch' sound**.

machine   chef   parachute   cheese   attach   beach

'ch' spells the 'sh' sound here.   'ch' spells the 'ch' sound here.

4) The letters **'tu'** can sometimes spell the **'ch' sound** too.

picture   actual   fortunate   century

The 'z' sound can be quite tricky to spell

Both **'z'** and **'s'** can spell the **'z' sound**.

A 'zz' or 'ss' can also spell the 'z' sound.

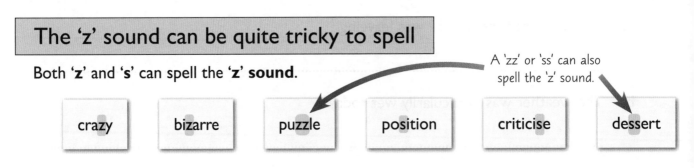

crazy   bizarre   puzzle   position   criticise   dessert

It's tricky to spell the 'zh' sound too

There are several ways to spell the **'zh' sound**.

Although 'sure' is pronounced with the 'sh' sound, it can make a 'zh' sound at the end of some words.

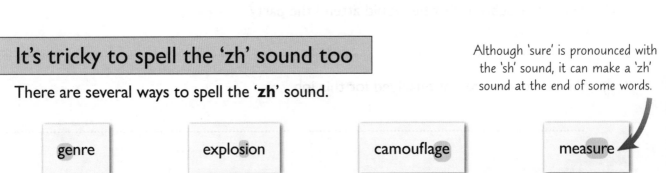

genre   explosion   camouflage   measure

Common Word Sounds

The letters 'ough' can sound very different

The letters '**ough**' are pronounced in many different ways.

though — 'ough' sounds like 'oh' here.

rough — 'ough' sounds like 'uff' here.

borough — 'ough' sounds like 'uh' here.

ought — 'ough' sounds like 'or' here.

cough — 'ough' sounds like 'off' here.

There are lots of ways to spell the long 'e' sound

The letters '**ee**', '**ea**' and '**ie**' are the most common ways to make the **long 'e' sound**.

breeze   committee   dream   weasel   piece   calorie

The letter 'c' can have a hard or soft sound

1) The **soft 'c' sound** is like an 's' sound.
    It is made when the letter '**c**' is followed by an '**e**', '**i**' or '**y**'.

distance   recent   medicine   exercise   frequency

2) The **hard 'c' sound** is like a 'k' sound. It's made when a '**c**' is followed
    by a letter **other** than 'e', 'i' or 'y', or is at the **end** of a word.

cross   according   scheme   backward   panic

There are several ways to spell the 'ks' sound

The '**ks**' **sound** can be tricky because there are lots of ways to spell it.

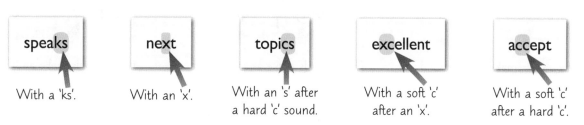

speaks — With a 'ks'.

next — With an 'x'.

topics — With an 's' after a hard 'c' sound.

excellent — With a soft 'c' after an 'x'.

accept — With a soft 'c' after a hard 'c'.

Common Word Sounds

The 'j' sound can be difficult to spell

You can spell the **'j' sound** with the letters **'j'**, **'g'**, **'d'**, **'ge'** or **'dge'**.

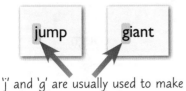

jump   giant

gradual

college   knowledge

'j' and 'g' are usually used to make the 'j' sound at the start of words.

'd' can be used to make the 'j' sound in the middle of words.

'ge' and 'dge' can be used to make the 'j' sound at the end of words.

It's tricky to spell words that end with an 'ul' sound

The **'ul' sound** is usually spelt by using the letters **'al'**, **'el'** or **'le'**.

musical   personal   squirrel   travel   example   available

There are a few ways to spell the hard 'g' sound

The **hard 'g' sound** can be spelt using the letters **'g'**, **'gu'** or **'gue'**.

grateful   wrong   figment   guarantee   guess   colleague

Vowels do not always sound how they are spelt

There are many words where the **vowel** isn't **spelt** how it is **said**.

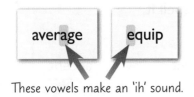

average   equip

curiosity   qualify

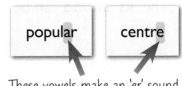

popular   centre

These vowels make an 'ih' sound.

These vowels make an 'oh' sound.

These vowels make an 'er' sound.

Practice Questions

1) Complete the words in the sentences below using the sound in brackets.

   a) I really appre...........iate you meeting with me today.   (sh)

   b) That restaurant makes an e...........ellent chicken stew.   (ks)

   c) Owen eats porri........... for breakfast every morning.   (j)

   d) The ch...........f had been in power for many years.   (long e)

   e) She gave me a necklace to mark the o...........asion.   (hard c)

   f) Ingrid wanted her visit to be a surpri...........e.   (z)

   g) The adven...........rer started his mission in Nepal.   (ch)

   h) Dominic has re...........ently started a training course.   (soft c)

   i) The newspaper artic........... was very interesting.   (ul)

   j) Carly is a security ....ard at a shopping centre.   (hard g)

   k) Please mention any relevant qu...........lifications.   (oh)

2) Each sentence below has a mistake. Rewrite the sentences with the mistake corrected.

   a) Althoh it was dark, she could see the shadows.

   ....

   b) I'll need to take your meazurements for the suit.

   ....

   c) Omar looked at the holiday broshure for ideas.

   ....

   d) I need to tidy up the guarden.

   ....

   e) We admire employies who are professional.

   ....

   f) Joanna thinks a healthy lifestyal is important.

   ....

Section Five — Using Correct Spelling

Common Word Endings

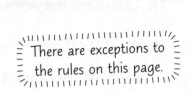

The 'shun' sound can be spelt in different ways

If a word has the '**shun**' sound added to the **end** of it,
the **last letter** of the root word normally decides how it is spelt.

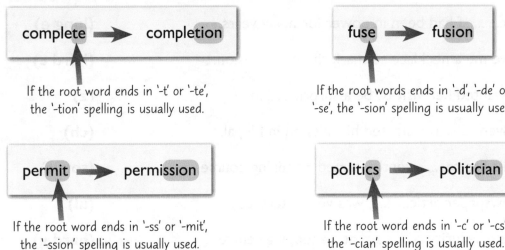

complete ➡ completion

If the root word ends in '-t' or '-te',
the '-tion' spelling is usually used.

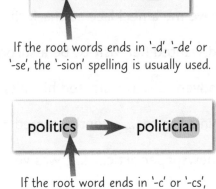

fuse ➡ fusion

If the root words ends in '-d', '-de' or
'-se', the '-sion' spelling is usually used.

permit ➡ permission

If the root word ends in '-ss' or '-mit',
the '-ssion' spelling is usually used.

politics ➡ politician

If the root word ends in '-c' or '-cs',
the '-cian' spelling is usually used.

There are a few ways to spell the 'shus' sound

The '**shus**' sound is normally spelt with either '**-tious**' or '**-cious**'.

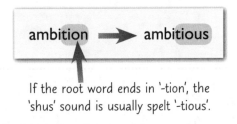

ambition ➡ ambitious

If the root word ends in '-tion', the
'shus' sound is usually spelt '-tious'.

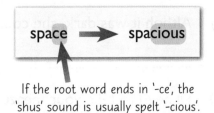

space ➡ spacious

If the root word ends in '-ce', the
'shus' sound is usually spelt '-cious'.

The spelling of the 'shul' sound can vary

1) You normally spell the '**shul**' sound with the letters '**-cial**' or '**-tial**'.

2) The '**-cial**' spelling is usually used after a **vowel**.

artificial   facial   social   special

3) The '**-tial**' spelling is usually used after a **consonant**.

essential   partial   influential   confidential

Practice Questions

1) Circle the correct word to complete each sentence.

   a) I have an appointment with the **optician / optision**.

   b) The **official / offitial** statement is that the fire has been put out.

   c) Gary's **operation / operasion** was a huge success.

   d) Harriet showed a great deal of **potential / potencial**.

   e) Dylan's dog was known for being **vitious / vicious**.

   f) Her **obsession / obsetion** with social media was worrying.

2) Add '**-tion**', '**-sion**', '**-ssion**' or '**-cian**' to make the words in brackets fit the sentence.

   a) This (inject) .... will protect you against the flu.

   b) Danielle gave Will a look of (confuse) ....

   c) Dominique hired a (magic) .... for her party.

   d) I have a (confess) .... to make.

   e) Grace was pleased about her (promote) .... at work.

   f) They had a (discuss) .... about climate change.

3) Each sentence below has a mistake. Rewrite the sentences with the mistakes corrected.

   a) Karl's behaviour was very suspitious.

   ....

   b) Femi signed a contract extention yesterday.

   ....

   c) Leanne's sesion with her therapist was useful.

   ....

   d) I'm afraid this disease is very infeccious.

   ....

Common Word Endings

Sometimes different word endings sound very similar

1) The '**-ant**' and '**-ent**' endings both sounds like '**unt**'.

| hesitant | observant | frequent | innocent |

2) The '**-ance**' and '**-ence**' endings both sound like '**unce**'.

| observance | ambulance | patience | innocence |

3) The '**-ancy**' and '**-ency**' endings both sound like '**uncy**'.

| vacancy | tenancy | currency | frequency |

Different endings make different types of words

You can add '**-ation**' to some words that end in '**ant**', '**ance**' or '**ancy**' to turn them into a **noun** that describes an **action**.

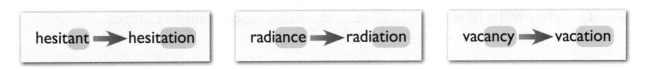

hesitant ➡ hesitation   radiance ➡ radiation   vacancy ➡ vacation

'-able' / '-ible' and '-ably' / '-ibly' all sound similar

1) Although these word endings sound similar, they are **spelt differently**.

2) '**-able**' and '**-ably**' are usually used when a **complete** root word can be heard before them.

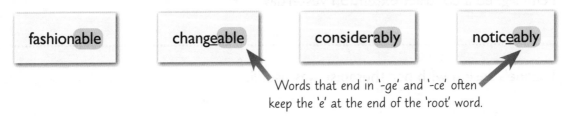

| fashionable | changeable | considerably | noticeably |

Words that end in '-ge' and '-ce' often keep the 'e' at the end of the 'root' word.

3) '**-ible**' and '**-ibly**' are usually used when you **can't** hear a **complete** root word before them.

| irresponsible | terrible | feasibly | possibly |

Practice Questions

1) Circle the correct word to complete each sentence.

   a) The roses are especially **fragrant** / **fragrent** during spring.

   b) The rehearsal for the play went **terrably** / **terribly**.

   c) Joy pushed the **emergancy** / **emergency** button.

   d) Emily's boss gave her an excellent **reference** / **referance**.

   e) Renata was almost **invisable** / **invisible** in the shadows.

   f) His **performance** / **performence** made everyone cry.

   g) Mason is very **independant** / **independent** for his age.

   h) The staff were threatened with **redundancy** / **redundency**.

   i) The contract seemed very **agreeable** / **agreeible** to Laurence.

2) Each sentence below has a mistake. Rewrite the sentences with the mistakes corrected.

   a) His confidance was almost arrogance.

   ....

   b) Her expression was defient and angry.

   ....

   c) Alicia regrettibly declined the invitation.

   ....

   d) Mushrooms have a horrable texture.

   ....

   e) Charity work is always incredibly admirible.

   ....

   f) Polly needed travel insurence for her holiday.

   ....

   g) I've just collected the keys to my new apartmant.

   ....

Common Spelling Mistakes

Words with double letters can be hard to spell

1) It's tricky to spell words with **double letters** because you **can't hear** the second letter when the word is said.

2) **Learn** how to spell **common** words with **double letters** like these ones:

different · tomorrow · professional · address

necessary · immediate · occasionally · success

Some words have more than one pair of double letters.

Silent letters can be tricky

1) Sometimes you **can't hear** a certain **letter** when you say a word.

2) These are known as **silent letters** — here are some examples:

when · listen · island · condemn · guarantee

write · could · doubt · knight · scientific

Unclear sounds make it hard to spell some words

1) Sometimes the **sound** in a word **isn't clear** — especially when it comes to **vowels**.

2) This can make them quite **difficult** to spell — here are some examples:

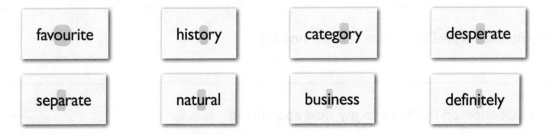

favourite · history · category · desperate

separate · natural · business · definitely

Practice Questions

1) Circle the correct word to complete each sentence.

    a)   I'm afraid I can't **guarantee / garantee** anything at this early stage.

    b)   The garage has been doing really good **busness / business** this year.

    c)   My parents used to **listen / lisen** to a lot of country music.

    d)   We only use **nateral / natural** materials in our products.

    e)   I **doubt / dout** I'll ever be able to afford a house in London.

    f)   Lily is **desperate / desparate** to go back to Italy this summer.

    g)   He wants to see you in his office **imediately / immediately**.

2) Each sentence below has a mistake. Rewrite the sentences with the mistakes corrected.

    a)   Your order may be ready to send tomorow.

    ....

    b)   You should definately apply for that job.

    ....

    c)   We chose a diffrent route to work today.

    ....

    d)   Wen are you going for dinner?

    ....

    e)   He bought me my faverite flowers.

    ....

    f)   I suceeded in persuading him.

    ....

    g)   Cud I drive the van?

    ....

    h)   We rote out the report.

    ....

Commonly Confused Words

Homophones can be quite tricky to spell

1) **Homophones** are words that are **pronounced the same**, but have **different meanings** and are **spelt differently**.

2) Make sure that you choose the **correct word** in your writing.

3) You need to know **all** of the **common homophones** on the word list. Some are below:

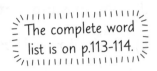
The complete word list is on p.113-114.

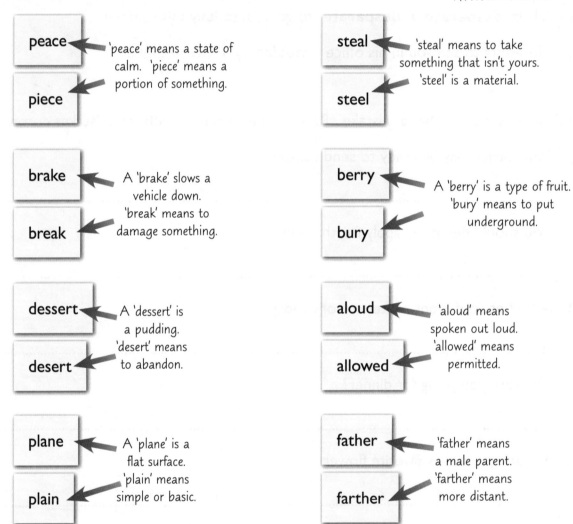

peace
'peace' means a state of calm. 'piece' means a portion of something.
piece

steal
'steal' means to take something that isn't yours. 'steel' is a material.
steel

brake
A 'brake' slows a vehicle down. 'break' means to damage something.
break

berry
A 'berry' is a type of fruit. 'bury' means to put underground.
bury

dessert
A 'dessert' is a pudding. 'desert' means to abandon.
desert

aloud
'aloud' means spoken out loud. 'allowed' means permitted.
allowed

plane
A 'plane' is a flat surface. 'plain' means simple or basic.
plain

father
'father' means a male parent. 'farther' means more distant.
farther

4) Some homophones are words that have been **shortened** by **apostrophes**.

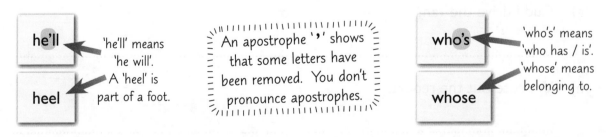

he'll
'he'll' means 'he will'. A 'heel' is part of a foot.
heel

An apostrophe ' ' ' shows that some letters have been removed. You don't pronounce apostrophes.

who's
'who's' means 'who has / is'. 'whose' means belonging to.
whose

Section Five — Using Correct Spelling

Commonly Confused Words

'Your' and 'you're' mean different things

1) **'Your'** means 'belonging to you'.

Keep your uniform in your locker. ← The uniform belongs to you.

2) **'You're'** means 'you are'.

You're working twice this week. ← If you can replace 'you're' with 'you are' and the sentence makes sense, then it's the right one.

Learn how to use 'to' and 'too'

1) **'To'** can mean 'towards', or it can be part of a **verb**.

'To' is often followed by a verb.

He's going to Spain. — When 'to' means 'towards', it's followed by a place.

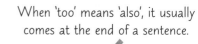

He's going to come at 6 pm.

2) **'Too'** can mean 'too much', or it can mean 'also'.

When 'too' means 'also', it usually comes at the end of a sentence.

This car is too slow. ← This version of 'too' often has a describing word after it.

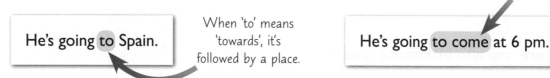

He enjoyed the play too.

Don't confuse 'know' and 'no'

1) **'Know'** means 'to be certain about something' or 'to be familiar with'.

I know where it is.

She knows my manager, Mr Onwe.

2) **'No'** means the opposite of yes.

No, I can't give you a lift home.

Commonly Confused Words

'Their', 'they're' and 'there' are all different

1) **'Their'** means 'belonging to them'.

> Their flat has two bedrooms.

> He took their warning seriously.

2) **'They're'** means 'they are'.

> They're living in a two-bed flat.

> They're giving him a warning.

If you can replace 'they're' with 'they are' and the sentence still makes sense, then it is right.

3) **'There'** is used to talk about a **place**.

> The flat is over there.

> They are there now.

4) **'There'** can also **introduce a sentence**.

> There is no reason to warn him.

> There are two choices.

'Are' and 'our' sound alike

1) **'Are'** is a **verb**.

> We are paid every Friday.

> Are we going out tonight?

2) **'Our'** means 'belonging to us'.

> Our house is near the church.

> It's our favourite song.

Practice Questions

1) Circle the correct word to complete each sentence.

   a)   We've booked a family holiday **to / too** the Alps.

   b)   **Our / Are** workshop is really messy at the moment.

   c)   My girlfriend's parents work at the hospital. **They're / Their** both nurses.

   d)   Did you know you have left **you're / your** lights on?

   e)   Can you tell me **who's / whose** house that is, please?

   f)   I did not **no / know** that the bank was open today.

2) Each sentence below has a mistake. Rewrite the sentences with the mistakes corrected.

   a)   Mr Clay is our honoured guessed tonight.

   ....

   b)   The driver did not see the sign their.

   ....

   c)   You're handbag is in the locker.

   ....

   d)   My favourite desert is apple pie with custard.

   ....

   e)   The breaks on the car squealed loudly.

   ....

   f)   Her dress is old-fashioned and very plane.

   ....

   g)   Heel be arriving at Victoria station in three hours.

   ....

Commonly Confused Words

'Bought' and 'brought' mean different things

'**Bought**' is the past tense of '**buy**'. '**Brought**' is the past tense of '**bring**'.

I bought an umbrella. ← This means 'I purchased an umbrella'.

I brought an umbrella. ← This means 'I carried an umbrella with me'.

'Been' and 'being' can sound the same

1) '**Been**' is used after the words '**have**', '**has**' or '**had**'.

I have been there before.

She has been too.

Tom had been before us both.

2) '**Being**' is used after '**am**', '**are**', '**were**' or '**was**'.

I am being careful.

They are being welcomed.

We were being friendly.

Josh was being protective.

'Teach' and 'learn' are opposites

1) You **teach** information **to** someone else.

2) You **learn** information **from** someone else.

I teach French to my sister.

My sister learns French from me.

Make sure you are using the right word

1) '**A lot**' means '**many**'. '**Alot**' is **not** a word.

2) '**Thank you**' is always written as **two words**.

3) '**Maybe**' means '**perhaps**'. '**May be**' means '**might be**'.

If you can swap in 'might be', then you're using the right version of 'may be'.

Maybe I'll come to the cinema.

He may be coming to the cinema.

Practice Questions

1) Circle the correct word to complete each sentence.

a) I have **been** / **being** thinking about going to university.

b) Adrian is **teaching** / **learning** how to play the piano.

c) My uncle **maybe** / **may be** coming to visit us.

d) Yvonne and Tabitha were **been** / **being** very immature.

e) Mr Cross **teaches** / **learns** thirty pupils in his German class.

f) Sina **bought** / **brought** the dog to her dad's house.

g) **Maybe** / **may be** I'll go to Spain next year.

h) I **taught** / **learned** how to knit from my grandmother.

i) You **maybe** / **may be** able to catch the train at 7 o'clock.

2) Each sentence below has a mistake. Rewrite the sentences with the mistakes corrected.

a) I haven't been to the gym alot this year.

....

b) He seemed honest, but may be he was just a good liar.

....

c) Having a baby learns parents lots of new skills.

....

d) Thankyou for having us this weekend.

....

e) It had being months since she had seen her friends.

....

f) You're been ridiculous — your outfit looks great.

....

g) Miriam bought cakes to the office.

....

Helpful Spelling Tips

The 'i' before 'e' rule

1) 'i' and 'e' often appear **next to each other** in a word.

2) This means it can be **tricky** to **remember** which comes **first**.

3) Use the **'i' before 'e' rule** to help:

'i' before 'e' except after 'c', but only when it rhymes with 'bee'.

The 'ie' sound rhymes with 'bee', so 'i' goes before 'e'.

The 'ie' sound rhymes with 'bee', but there's a 'c', so the 'e' goes before 'i'.

The 'ie' sound doesn't rhyme with 'bee', so 'e' goes before 'i'.

The 'ie' sound comes after 'c', but it doesn't rhyme with 'bee', so 'i' goes before 'e'.

A few words don't follow the rule

Watch out for these **tricky examples**.

In these words, the 'ei' sound does rhyme with 'bee', but the 'e' still goes before the 'i'.

The 'i' goes before the 'e', even though it comes after 'c' and rhymes with 'bee'.

Make up phrases to help you spell tricky words

Make up **sentences** or **phrases** to remind you how words are spelt.

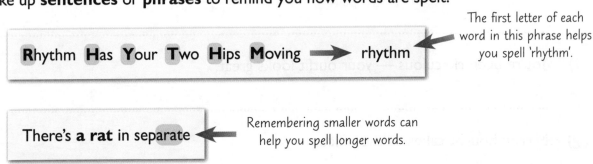

Rhythm **H**as **Y**our **T**wo **H**ips **M**oving → rhythm

The first letter of each word in this phrase helps you spell 'rhythm'.

There's **a rat** in separate

Remembering smaller words can help you spell longer words.

Practice Questions

1) Rewrite each word so it is spelt correctly.

   a) breif ....

   b) wieght ....

   c) peice ....

   d) nieghbour ....

   e) recieve ....

   f) feild ....

2) These four words can be tricky to spell. Write down a phrase underneath each word to help you remember how to spell it.

   | because |

   ....

   ....

   | could |

   ....

   ....

   | weird |

   ....

   ....

   | height |

   ....

   ....

Different Types of Question

You will have several tasks to do in the writing test

1) You might be asked to put some words in **alphabetical order**.

2) You could have a **grammar** or **punctuation** task to complete —
   for example, you might have to change **singular words** into **plurals**.

3) You will have **two** different **writing tasks** — each task should tell you how much to write.

4) You will also have a multiple choice **spelling test**.

5) You will have **50 minutes** to complete **all** of the tasks.

Be careful when ordering words alphabetically

Turn to p.66 for more about ordering words alphabetically.

1) Make sure you can order words according to the **position** of their letters in the **alphabet**.

2) If two or more words start with the **same letter**, look at the letter in the **next** place along.

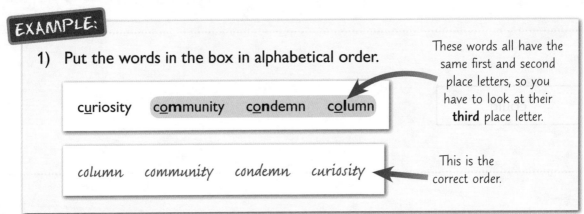

EXAMPLE:

1) Put the words in the box in alphabetical order.

curiosity   community   condemn   column

*These words all have the same first and second place letters, so you have to look at their **third** place letter.*

column   community   condemn   curiosity

This is the correct order.

You might have to make words plural

You'll need to show you can turn **singular** words into **plurals** — including **irregular** plurals.

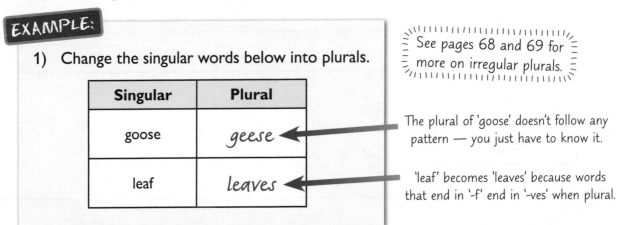

EXAMPLE:

1) Change the singular words below into plurals.

See pages 68 and 69 for more on irregular plurals.

Singular	Plural
goose	geese
leaf	leaves

The plural of 'goose' doesn't follow any pattern — you just have to know it.

'leaf' becomes 'leaves' because words that end in '-f' end in '-ves' when plural.

Different Types of Question

There will be two longer writing tasks in your writing test

1) These tasks will test you on your **writing ability**, as well as your **spelling**, **punctuation** and **grammar**.

There's more about this on the next page.

2) You will be told the **types of text** you need to write and **who** you are writing them for, e.g. a **letter** to a **friend**.

3) You should get a few **bullet points** to tell you **what** you need to write about.

4) You may also be told how many **sentences** or **paragraphs** you need to write.

EXAMPLE:

1) You buy a cake from a shop but realise that it is mouldy when you get home. Write a letter of complaint to the shop about what has happened.

This tells you what text you have to write and who you need to write to.

You should include:

- what the problem is

- when you bought the cake

- what you want the shop to do about it.

The bullet points tell you what you need to write about.

Write at least 5 sentences. This tells you how much you need to write.

You will have to answer some spelling questions

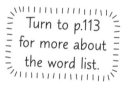Turn to p.113 for more about the word list.

1) You need to show that you can **spell** a range of words **correctly**.

2) **Most** of the words in the spelling test should come from the **word list**.

3) There will be an **incomplete** sentence and a **list of words** next to it.

4) You'll need to choose the word that is spelt **correctly** to **complete** the sentence.

EXAMPLE:

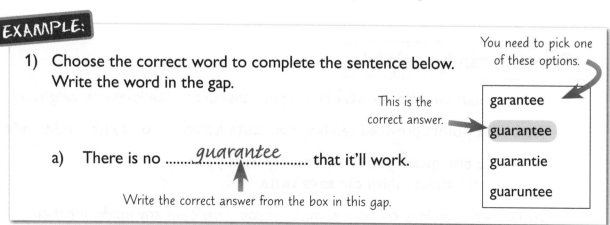

1) Choose the correct word to complete the sentence below. Write the word in the gap.

You need to pick one of these options.

This is the correct answer.

a) There is no ......*guarantee*...... that it'll work.

Write the correct answer from the box in this gap.

garantee
guarantee
guarantie
guaruntee

Advice for the Writing Test

Read the question carefully before you start

1) There will be information in the **question** to help you think of what to write.

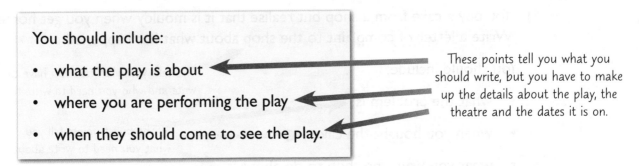

1) You are organising a play with your drama club.
Write an email to invite your friends to see it.

You have to write an email inviting your friends to see the play you are organising.

2) The **bullet points** under the question tell you what to write.

3) However, there isn't just **one right answer** to a writing question.

You should include:

- what the play is about

- where you are performing the play

- when they should come to see the play.

These points tell you what you should write, but you have to make up the details about the play, the theatre and the dates it is on.

4) Everything you write should **link** to the **question**. Don't write anything that **isn't relevant**.

Make sure you divide your time carefully

1) Make sure you leave enough **time** to complete **all** of the tasks you have to do.

2) If you get stuck on any of the **shorter questions**, move on and **come back** to them if you have time.

3) You will have two **longer writing tasks** — if one of these is worth **more marks**, spend a bit **more time** on that one.

4) Leave time to answer the **spelling questions** — they can be quick marks to pick up.

Planning can be helpful

1) A **quick plan** can help you **structure** your answers to the longer writing tasks.

2) The **bullet points** provided can help you **start** a plan — you'll just need to **add details**.

3) Following a plan means you know **exactly** what you want to write about, which can **save time**.

4) **Don't** spend too long on plans though — you **won't** get any marks for them.

Advice for the Writing Test

Learn the word list before your writing test

1) There are **several words** you could be asked to **spell correctly** in the writing test.

2) They can be found in the **word list** on pages 113 and 114 of this book.

3) **Any** of these **words** could come up in **any** of the **tasks** for the writing test.

Take care with spelling, punctuation and grammar

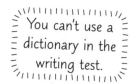
You can't use a dictionary in the writing test.

1) You will be marked on your **spelling**, **punctuation** and **grammar** in the longer writing tasks.

2) When you write a word that is in the **question**, make sure you spell it correctly.

3) If you don't know how to spell a word, **reword** your sentence so you don't use it.

way I was treated

I would like to complain about the ~~service I recieved~~ when I bought a bag from your shop last week.

If you don't know how to spell 'received', you can change the sentence so you don't have to write it.

Make sure you know the grammar and punctuation rules on pages 50 to 65.

Think about format, language and content

1) Write in **full sentences** and **use paragraphs correctly**.

2) Make sure that you use language that is **appropriate** for the **person you're addressing** and the **reason you're writing**.

3) Always keep your writing **polite**, even if you're writing to complain about something.

4) **Don't** use words like 'coz' or 'tho', even if you are writing to a friend.

5) Make sure you write about **everything** that you are asked to.

Checking your work is important

1) If you have time at the end of the test, **check** your work for mistakes.

2) Make sure your answers **make sense**.

3) Check your **spelling**, **punctuation** and **grammar**.

Candidate Surname	Candidate Forename(s)

Date	Candidate Signature

Functional Skills

English   Entry Level 3

Writing

Time allowed: 50 minutes

You **may not** use a dictionary.

Instructions to candidates
- Use **black or blue ink** to write your answers.
- Write your name and the date in the spaces provided above.
- Answer each question in the spaces provided.

Information for candidates
- There are **36 marks** available for this paper.
- There are marks for **spelling**, **punctuation** and **grammar**.

Advice to candidates
- Read each question carefully before you start answering it.
- Make sure your answers are written clearly.
- If you have time, **check** your answers at the end.

Total Marks

1   Put the words from the box below in **alphabetical order**.

thread	thirsty	theatre	thumb

....

....

....

....

(1 mark)

2   Change the singular words below into plurals.

Singular	Plural
sky	
tooth	

(2 marks)

3 You are organising a family party to celebrate your parents' 30th wedding anniversary.

Write a letter to a family member inviting them to come.

You should include:

- the date and time of the party
- where the party will be
- what to wear to the party.

You must format your letter correctly.

Aim to write **at least 5** sentences.

Write your letter on the next page.

4   A new animal shelter has opened in your local area.

Write an email to the manager asking to join their team of volunteers.

You should include:

- why you are emailing them

- why you would like to join the team

- any relevant skills you have

- when you are available to help.

You must include a **subject**.

Aim to write **8 or more sentences**. You must use joining words
to write at least **3 compound sentences**.

Write at least **2 paragraphs**.

	To:	hartleyfordshelter@azmail.co.uk
Send	Subject:	

....

....

....

....

....

....

....

....

....

....

....

....

....

....

....

....

....

....

....

....

....

....

....

....

....

....

....

....

....

(14 marks)

Writing Practice Paper

5 **Complete each sentence by choosing the correct word from the box.**
Write the word you choose in the gap provided.

| compitition |
| competition |
| computition |
| competishun |

Example

I have entered the cookery <u>competition</u>.

| frequentlie |
| freequently |
| frequently |
| frequantly |

a) I have to practise playing the piano ....

| achieve |
| acheeve |
| acheive |
| acheave |

b) What do you want to .... in this job?

| shugar |
| suger |
| shuger |
| sugar |

c) I take milk and one .... in my tea.

| rough |
| ruff |
| rouf |
| ruogh |

d) This dress is made of a very .... fabric.

| scene |
| seen |
| sceen |
| sean |

e) It was the fastest car I'd ever ....

f) My favourite season is ....

| autum |
| autumn |
| aurtumn |
| autumm |

g) The knives are made from stainless ....

| steal |
| stiel |
| steel |
| steell |

h) My older sister works in ....

| educacian |
| educasion |
| educassion |
| education |

i) I ate every single .... of that cake.

| crum |
| crumb |
| crumm |
| crumn |

j) We will order .... after our main course.

| deserrt |
| desert |
| dessert |
| desertt |

(10 marks)

TOTAL FOR PAPER = 36 MARKS

Additional Writing Space

Answers

Part 1 — Reading

Section One — Finding Information in Texts

Page 5

Q1 a — A swimming club
Q2 c — Tells you about cycling
Q3 b — Advertises a cleaning job
Q4 d — An internet café

Page 7

Q1 b — The last 5 years
Q2 c — The council
Q3 September
Q4 At rush hour
Q5 Visit the website

Page 9

Q1 Answers may vary, e.g.:
- To do with a position of authority
- Acting on behalf of an organisation

Q2 b — Stated
Q3 a — Noun
Q4 Answers may vary, e.g.:
- Able to be depended on
- Trustworthy

Page 11

Q1 c — Working as a on-call firefighter
Q2 b — To give cookie-making instructions

Page 15

Q1 c — You can take a cruise at 11.30 in June.
Q2 Answers may vary, e.g.:
- To make it stand out
- To show that it's important information

Q3 • The coastline
- The wildlife

Q4 b — Click the 'Wildlife' tab
d — Click the link on the word 'wildlife'

Reading Practice Paper

Text A (Page 23)

Q1 B — To tell you how to grow herbs

Q2 B — In a bright place
Q3 C — Enough
Q4 Enough to cover them
Q5 • Thyme
- Parsley

Q6 • The back of the seed packet
- Gardening websites

Text B (Page 25)

Q7 C — Quotes include all costs.
Q8 C — Moves for old people
Q9 B — Replace the item
Q10 D — Undamaged
Q11 • Calling them
- Emailing them
- Visiting their office

Q12 You could write any one of these:
- Careful
- Thorough
- Supportive

Text C (Page 27)

Q13 A — Fill in an application form
Q14 D — Personality
Q15 Read the instructions
Q16 • It will help you avoid making basic mistakes.
- It will help you to make a good first impression.

Q17 • A recent employer
- A teacher
- A tutor

Part 2 — Writing

Section One — What to Write About

Page 29

Q1 a) The council
b) Your friends
c) Your electricity supplier
d) The whole company

Q2 a) To ask if you can paint your house
b) To tell people how to sponsor you
c) To complain about your delayed flight
d) To offer to volunteer

Page 31

Q1 a — Hi Aunt Milly, I love the beautiful photo album you sent me. Thanks so much.

Q2 b — I am applying for the childcare assistant position. I have lots of childcare experience.

Q3 a — Dear John, I would like to request two weeks of annual leave at the end of August.

Q4 b — Hi Dave, I'm so sorry I didn't get in touch this weekend.

Q5 An email to invite people to your friend's party.
Chatty

Q6 A letter to complain about your recent hotel stay.
Serious

Q7 A leaflet to advertise your cleaning business.
Serious

Q8 An email to ask your landlord to fix your gate.
Serious

Q9 A letter to inform your grandma about your holiday.
Chatty

Page 33

Q1 a — Bookshelf for sale. It's two metres tall and made of oak. It's a great deal at £30.

Q2 c — Yesterday, a late train made me late for work. I would like a refund.

Q3 b — The main road needs resurfacing. It is a busy road, and there are many potholes.

Page 35

Q1 a) Say that you want to apply for the course
b) Talk about the skills and experience you have
c) Say how the course would be helpful for your future

Q2 a) Tell them about the cake stall
b) Ask them to bake some cakes
c) Tell them when the cakes should be ready by

Q3 a) Say you would like to use the room for your course
b) Give details of when you would like to use the room
c) Say how the course would be good for the community

Page 37

Q1 You need to show that you have started a new paragraph by leaving a space at the beginning of the first line, or by leaving a line. Here is what you should have written:

People all over the world celebrate the start of the new year. They count the seconds until midnight on the 31st of December, to mark the start of a new calendar year.

Hogmanay is a Scottish celebration which is also held on the 31st of December. Some people carry on the celebrations until the 2nd of January, which is also a bank holiday in Scotland.

Chinese New Year falls on a different date each year, and is celebrated in at least nine countries. The festivities last for around two weeks.

Page 39

Q1 Answers may vary, for example:
Heading: Gardening with Grace
Subheading: My services
Bullet points:
• Lawn mowing
• Hedge cutting
• General garden maintenance
• Planting services
• Landscaping evaluations
Subheading: Prices
Subheading: Contact me

Section Two — Different Types of Writing

Page 41

Q1 Your letter should:
• Use full sentences.
• Start with 'Dear Sir or Madam' because you do not know who you are writing to.
• End with 'Yours faithfully' and your name.

You should include:
• Why you think the new bus service is a good idea. For example, 'many people rely on the bus to travel around town', 'it will give people more travel options', or 'the new service would encourage more people to use the bus'.
• When you think the new buses should run. For example, 'on the weekends' or 'late at night'.
• Who you think would use them. For example, 'shift workers, young people and people who cannot drive'.

Page 43

Q1 In your email:
• Write Steff's email address 'steffburns@azmail.co.uk' in the 'To' box.
• Write what the email is about in the 'Subject' box.
• Write your email in full sentences.
• Start with a greeting like 'Hello Steff'.
• End with a sign-off like 'Best wishes'.

You should include:
• What you would like to see on the new menu. For example, 'more vegetarian food'.
• How often you buy food from the canteen. For example, 'I buy lunch every Friday'.

Page 45

Q1 The first three boxes on the application form only need short answers. For example, 'Ruth Riley', '02/05/87' and 'Customer Service Assistant'.
For the longer answer you should write in full sentences.

Under 'Why are you right for this job?' you should include:
• Why you would like the job. For example, 'I would like to improve my customer service skills'.
• Any work experience you have. For example, 'I have worked in a shop'.

• What other useful skills you have. For example, 'I am good at dealing with problems' or 'I am good at talking to people'.

Page 47

Q1 Here is an example of what you could write:
• Decide where to put your shelf.
• Mark the wall to show where you want to put the brackets.
• Use a spirit level to make sure that the brackets will be level.
• Drill holes into the wall for the screws.
• Screw the brackets to the walls.
• Screw the shelves to the brackets.
• Check the shelves are secure.

Page 49

Q1 Your report should be written in full sentences.
You should divide your writing into sections. For example:
• 'This Year's Charity Day', including what happened on the day.
• 'Money Raised', including how much money was raised this year, and whether it was any more than last year.
• 'What the money is for', including what the hospital will spend the money on.

Section Three — Using Grammar

Page 51

Q1 a) Our manager <u>writes</u> the timetable.
b) My neighbour <u>organised</u> a party.
c) I <u>applied</u> for the job today.
d) We <u>eat</u> our lunch in the canteen.
e) At college I <u>studied</u> engineering.

Q2 a) The <u>car</u> broke down on the way to work.
b) Our <u>cat</u> caught a mouse.
c) <u>You</u> cycled to work last week.
d) <u>I</u> read the application form.
e) My <u>sister</u> works in a bank.

Q3 Here is an example of what you could write:

The computer course will start at 9 am and finish at 5 pm. There will be a lunch break at 1 pm and two coffee breaks. Bring a pen and a notebook with you.

Page 53

Q1 a) The college offers childcare courses, <u>and</u> it organises work placements.

b) She was late for work <u>because</u> her alarm did not go off.

c) I want to buy a bike <u>so</u> I can get fit.

d) They went to the shop, <u>but</u> it had already closed.

e) You should try this tea <u>because</u> it is lovely.

f) I will either borrow the blue shoes, <u>or</u> buy the pink shoes.

g) He built the cupboard carefully, <u>but</u> it was still a bit wobbly.

h) At the park, we saw Ryan, <u>and</u> he had his new dog with him.

i) Bridget didn't know if she should go for a run, <u>or</u> go swimming.

Q2 Answers may vary, for example:

a) I am not feeling very well.

b) I can drive to work.

c) she did not like the old colour.

d) the sink has flooded.

e) I could go for a walk.

f) they were too short.

g) we can both come.

h) he could pay you back.

Page 55

Q1 a) specific

b) general

c) specific

d) general

e) specific

Q2 a) a

b) an

c) a

d) an

e) a

f) an

Q3 a) <u>The</u> spider in my room in huge.

b) There was <u>an</u> unusual smell in the kitchen.

c) She couldn't see because <u>the</u> sun was in her eyes.

d) <u>The</u> Managing Director of the company came to my party.

e) When I was in Japan, there was <u>a</u> big earthquake.

f) They wished they'd gone to <u>a</u> different hotel.

g) Leslie decided he was going to buy a puppy at <u>the</u> weekend.

Page 59

Q1 a) past

b) present

c) future

d) present

e) future

Q2 a) cooked

b) writes

c) washed

d) were

e) are

Q3 a) I <u>bought</u> four tomatoes but they were rotten.

b) We <u>were</u> at football yesterday.

c) I <u>caught</u> the train, but I was still late.

d) You <u>are</u> going to go to the beach tomorrow.

e) They <u>went</u> to a meeting yesterday.

Page 61

Q1 a) The children <u>play</u> in the park.

b) The fire alarm <u>rings</u> on Tuesdays.

c) She <u>walks</u> to the shops every day.

d) I <u>throw</u> away the bananas.

Q2 a) I could <u>have</u> done it yesterday, but I forgot.

b) You should <u>have</u> come to the party.

c) They <u>have</u> done the shopping already.

Section Four — Using Correct Punctuation

Page 63

Q1 a) <u>S</u>omebody stop that bus<u>!</u>

b) <u>M</u>y manager said <u>I</u> could take the day off<u>.</u>

c) <u>W</u>ho should <u>I</u> write a letter to<u>?</u>

d) <u>L</u>ook how bright the sun is today<u>!</u>

e) <u>W</u>ould you like to join our tennis club<u>?</u>

f) <u>W</u>e want to go to <u>C</u>ornwall for our holiday<u>.</u>

g) <u>D</u>oes this train go directly from <u>P</u>ortsmouth to <u>Y</u>ork?

h) <u>I</u> am going to the cinema with <u>A</u>nita tonight<u>.</u>

Page 65

Q1 a) It would be nice to visit Paris<u>,</u> Rome or Madrid.

b) He has a week off work<u>,</u> so he's going to relax.

c) I'm going shopping today<u>,</u> and I'm going swimming tomorrow.

d) The dish needs three potatoes<u>,</u> one onion<u>,</u> two peppers and four eggs.

e) They had planned to go hiking<u>,</u> but it was raining.

f) Jasmine<u>,</u> Elijah and Alex are too ill to come to work today.

g) They had strawberries<u>,</u> apples<u>,</u> pears and mangoes for sale.

h) The cinema was closed<u>,</u> so we went to the park.

i) Employees should be punctual<u>,</u> reliable and hard-working.

j) Lisa is getting married<u>,</u> and Tonya is her bridesmaid.

k) They were going to go on holiday<u>,</u> but their flight was cancelled.

l) We saw penguins<u>,</u> sea lions and elephants at the zoo.

Q2 a) It was a beautiful day, <u>so</u> Ollie went to the beach.

b) Jade's car broke down, <u>and</u> the bus was cancelled.

c) Liam wanted to get tickets, <u>but</u> they were sold out.

d) Emily's phone was stolen, <u>so</u> she called the police.

e) The weather forecast predicted rain, <u>but</u> it's sunny.

Section Five — Using Correct Spelling

Page 67

Q1 a) Abigail, Geoffrey, Richard, Samantha

b) books, picture, radio, television

c) across, badger, obsession, popular

d) native, network, nought, nugget

e) market, merchant, million, mountain

f) familiar, fiction, formal, frequent

g) secure, separate, serve, settlement
h) jealous, jersey, jester, jewel
i) cabbage, canopy, carnival, category
j) telephone, terrace, transport, trumpet
k) occupy, official, opening, opportunity
l) danger, desert, dolphin, double

Page 69
Q1 a) plant<u>s</u>
b) boy<u>s</u>
c) sandwich<u>es</u>
d) hal<u>ves</u>
e) countr<u>ies</u>
f) <u>feet</u>
Q2 a) The <u>loaves</u> of bread I bought were too hard.
b) Can <u>children</u> eat at your restaurant?
c) There are lots of <u>geese</u> by the lake today.
d) I talked about my <u>hobbies</u> in the interview.

Page 71
Q1 a) disagree
b) unpack
c) mismatch
d) informal
Q2 a) She is the <u>co-owner</u> of the company.
b) The instructions were <u>unnecessary</u>.
c) She needs to <u>re-evaluate</u> her choices.
d) He wished he could be <u>immortal</u>.
e) The two brothers were not <u>dissimilar</u>.
f) She <u>mistrusted</u> every word that he said.

Page 73
Q1 a) certainly
b) purposeful
c) user
d) supplied
e) loneliness
f) making
Q2 a) A <u>developer</u> is inspecting the house today.
b) The king was a very <u>merciful</u> ruler.
c) The stale sponge cake was <u>crumbly</u> and dry.

d) She <u>tried</u> to phone the call centre again.
e) His <u>laziness</u> isn't very professional.
Q3 a) I remembered the file as I was <u>leaving</u>.
b) The weather was <u>particularly</u> wet today.
c) She was <u>doubtful</u> that he would attend the party.
d) I'm afraid you are not <u>qualified</u> for this job.

Page 77
Q1 a) I really appre<u>ci</u>ate you meeting with me today.
b) That restaurant makes an ex<u>c</u>ellent chicken stew.
c) Owen eats porri<u>dg</u>e for breakfast every morning.
d) The ch<u>ie</u>f had been in power for many years.
e) She gave me a necklace to mark the o<u>cc</u>asion.
f) Ingrid wanted her visit to be a surpri<u>s</u>e.
g) The adven<u>tur</u>er started his mission in Nepal.
h) Dominic has re<u>c</u>ently started a training course.
i) The newspaper arti<u>c</u>le was very interesting.
j) Carly is a security <u>g</u>uard at a shopping centre.
k) Please mention any relevant qualifications.
Q2 a) <u>Although</u> it was dark, she could see the shadows.
b) I'll need to take your <u>measurements</u> for the suit.
c) Omar looked at the holiday <u>brochure</u> for ideas.
d) I need to tidy up the <u>garden</u>.
e) We admire <u>employees</u> who are professional.
f) Joanna thinks a healthy <u>lifestyle</u> is important.

Page 79
Q1 a) I have an appointment with the <u>optician</u>.
b) The <u>official</u> statement is that the fire has been put out.
c) Gary's <u>operation</u> was a huge success.
d) Harriet showed a great deal of <u>potential</u>.
e) Dylan's dog was known for being <u>vicious</u>.

f) Her <u>obsession</u> with social media was worrying.
Q2 a) This injec<u>tion</u> will protect you against the flu.
b) Danielle gave Will a look of confu<u>sion</u>.
c) Dominique hired a magi<u>cian</u> for her party.
d) I have a confe<u>ssion</u> to make.
e) Grace was pleased about her promo<u>tion</u> at work.
f) They had a discu<u>ssion</u> about climate change.
Q3 a) Karl's behaviour was very <u>suspicious</u>.
b) Femi signed a contract <u>extension</u> yesterday.
c) Leanne's <u>session</u> with her therapist was useful.
d) I'm afraid this disease is very infec<u>tious</u>.

Page 81
Q1 a) The roses are especially <u>fragrant</u> during spring.
b) The rehearsal for the play went <u>terribly</u>.
c) Joy pushed the <u>emergency</u> button.
d) Emily's boss gave her an excellent <u>reference</u>.
e) Renata was almost <u>invisible</u> in the shadows.
f) His <u>performance</u> made everyone cry.
g) Mason is very <u>independent</u> for his age.
h) The staff were threatened with <u>redundancy</u>.
i) The contract seemed very <u>agreeable</u> to Laurence.
Q2 a) His confid<u>ence</u> was almost arrogance.
b) Her expression was defi<u>ant</u> and angry.
c) Alicia regrett<u>ably</u> declined the invitation.
d) Mushrooms have a horr<u>ible</u> texture.
e) Charity work is always incredibly admir<u>able</u>.
f) Polly needed travel insur<u>ance</u> for her holiday.
g) I've just collected the keys to my new apart<u>ment</u>.

Page 83

Q1 a) I'm afraid I can't <u>guarantee</u> anything at this early stage.

b) The garage has been doing really good <u>business</u> this year.

c) My parents used to <u>listen</u> to a lot of country music.

d) We only use <u>natural</u> materials in our products.

e) I <u>doubt</u> I'll ever be able to afford a house in London.

f) Lily is <u>desperate</u> to go back to Italy this summer.

g) He wants to see you in his office <u>immediately</u>.

Q2 a) Your order may be ready to send <u>tomorrow</u>.

b) You should <u>definitely</u> apply for that job.

c) We chose a <u>different</u> route to work today.

d) <u>When</u> are you going for dinner?

e) He bought me my <u>favourite</u> flowers.

f) I <u>succeeded</u> in persuading him.

g) <u>Could</u> I drive the van?

h) We <u>wrote</u> out the report.

Page 87

Q1 a) We've booked a family holiday <u>to</u> the Alps.

b) <u>Our</u> workshop is really messy at the moment.

c) My girlfriend's parents work at the hospital. <u>They're</u> both nurses.

d) Did you know you have left <u>your</u> lights on.

e) Can you tell me <u>whose</u> house that is, please.

f) I did not <u>know</u> that the bank was open today.

Q2 a) Mr Clay is our honoured <u>guest</u> tonight.

b) The driver did not see the sign <u>there</u>.

c) <u>Your</u> handbag is in the locker.

d) My favourite <u>desert</u> is apple pie with custard.

e) The <u>brakes</u> on the car squealed loudly.

f) Her dress is old-fashioned and very <u>plain</u>.

g) <u>He'll</u> be arriving at Victoria station in three hours.

Page 89

Q1 a) I have <u>been</u> thinking about going to university.

b) Adrian is <u>learning</u> how to play the piano.

c) My uncle <u>may be</u> coming to visit us.

d) Yvonne and Tabitha were <u>being</u> very immature.

e) Mr Cross <u>teaches</u> thirty pupils in his German class.

f) Sina <u>brought</u> the dog to her dad's house.

g) <u>Maybe</u> I'll go to Spain next year.

h) I <u>learned</u> how to knit from my grandmother.

i) You <u>may be</u> able to catch the train at 7 o'clock.

Q2 a) I haven't been to the gym <u>a lot</u> this year.

b) He seemed honest, but <u>maybe</u> he was just a good liar.

c) Having a baby <u>teaches</u> parents lots of new skills.

d) <u>Thank you</u> for having us this weekend.

e) It had <u>been</u> months since she had seen her friends.

f) You're <u>being</u> ridiculous — your outfit looks great.

g) Miriam <u>brought</u> cakes to the office.

Page 91

Q1 a) brief

b) weight

c) piece

d) neighbour

e) receive

f) field

Q2 Answers will vary, for example:
Because = <u>B</u>ig <u>E</u>lephants <u>C</u>an <u>A</u>lways <u>U</u>nderstand <u>S</u>mall <u>E</u>lephants.
Could = <u>C</u>ows <u>O</u>nly <u>U</u>se <u>L</u>arge <u>D</u>oors.
Weird = <u>W</u>ooden <u>E</u>lephants <u>I</u>n <u>R</u>ed <u>D</u>resses.
Height = <u>H</u>appy <u>E</u>mily <u>I</u>s <u>G</u>etting <u>H</u>er <u>T</u>rain.

Writing Practice Paper

Question 1 (Page 97)
The correct order is:
• theatre
• thirsty
• thread
• thumb

Question 2 (Page 97)

Singular	Plural
sky	<u>skies</u>
tooth	<u>teeth</u>

Question 3 (Page 98)
There are 6 marks available for how you write your answer.
A top-level answer will:
• Communicate the information clearly using a chatty but polite style.
• Use an appropriate format and structure.
• Use language that is appropriate for the audience and purpose.

There are 3 marks available for the spelling, punctuation and grammar of your answer.
A top-level answer will:
• Use grammar and punctuation correctly and with few errors.
• Spell words correctly and with few errors.

Your letter should include:
• A date and a time for the party, e.g. '7 pm on 1st June'.
• Where the party will be, e.g. 'The Buttercup Hotel'.
• What to wear to the party, e.g. 'The party will have a formal dress code.'

You should set your letter out correctly:
• Address the recipient correctly, e.g. 'Hi Mary'.
• End the letter appropriately, e.g. 'Best wishes'.

Your letter should have a clear structure:
• Start with the purpose of the letter, e.g. 'I am writing to invite you to...'
• Go on to say when and where the party is taking place and what to wear to the party.
• End with what you want them to do, e.g. 'Please let me know if you can make it.'
• Use full sentences.

Question 4 (Page 100)

There are 10 marks available for how you write your answer.
A top-level answer will:
- Communicate the information clearly using a formal and polite style.
- Be long enough for the intended purpose and audience.
- Use an appropriate format and structure, including paragraphs.
- Use language that is appropriate for the audience and purpose.
- Use a range of sentence types accurately.

There are 4 marks available for the spelling, punctuation and grammar of your answer.
A top-level answer will:
- Use grammar and punctuation correctly and with few errors.
- Spell words correctly and with few errors.

Your email should include:
- An appropriate subject, e.g. 'Volunteer application'.
- Why you are emailing, e.g. 'I am writing to ask if I can join your team of volunteers.'
- Why you would like to join the team, e.g. 'I have always loved animals.'
- Any relevant skills you have, e.g. 'I used to work on a farm, so I am used to looking after animals.'
- When you are available to help, e.g. 'I would be happy to volunteer in the evening or at weekends.'

You should set your email out correctly:
- In the 'Subject' box, write a suitable subject, e.g. 'Volunteer Application'.
- Start with 'Dear Sir / Madam' because you don't know who you're writing to.
- End the email with 'Yours faithfully'.

Your email should have a clear and logical structure:
- Start by explaining the purpose of the email, e.g. 'I am getting in touch to ask...'
- Go on to explain why you would like to join the team, why you would be suitable for the job and when you would be able to volunteer.
- End with what you want them to do, e.g. 'I look forward to hearing from you soon.'
- Use paragraphs and full sentences. Start a new paragraph for each point.

Question 5 (Page 102)
a)   I have to practise playing the piano <u>frequently</u>.
b)   What do you want to <u>achieve</u> in this job?
c)   I take milk and one <u>sugar</u> in my tea.
d)   This dress is made of a very <u>rough</u> fabric.
e)   It was the fastest car I'd ever <u>seen</u>.
f)   My favourite season is <u>autumn</u>.
g)   The knives are made from stainless <u>steel</u>.
h)   My older sister works in <u>education</u>.
i)   I ate every single <u>crumb</u> of that cake.
j)   We will order <u>dessert</u> after our main course.

Glossary

Article

A piece of writing in a newspaper or magazine.

Bullet points

A way of breaking up information into separate points in a list.

Compound Sentence

A sentence that's made up of more than one simple sentence, connected by a joining word.

Contents

A list of the sections in a book.

Email

A message sent over the internet.

Form

A text which is made up of questions with spaces for you to write your answers in.

Glossary

A part of a text which explains the meaning of difficult words.

Grammar

Rules that you follow so your writing makes sense. For example, you should write 'she makes' instead of 'she make'.

Greeting

A phrase used to start a letter or email. For example, 'Dear Mr Brockton' or 'Hello everyone'.

Homophones

Words that are pronounced the same, but have different meanings and are spelt differently.

Index

A list of a text's main topics in alphabetical order, usually found at the back or end of the text.

Instructions

A list of sentences that tell you how to do something.

Joining word

A word like 'and' or 'because' that joins parts of a sentence together.

Key words

The most important words in a sentence or a text. They tell you what the writing is mainly about.

Layout

How a text is presented on the page using things like subheadings and tables.

Leaflet

A text, which is usually given away for free, that tells the reader about something.

Letter

A text written to a person, or a group of people, which is sent in the post.

Menu

A list which gives you the titles of the different pages of a website.

Paragraph

A group of sentences that are about the same thing.

Past tense

Writing that talks about something that has already happened.

Personal statement

A piece of writing about yourself, usually to apply for a job or a college course.

Plural

The form of a word that refers to more than one of something.

Prefixes

Letters added to the start of a word which change the word's meaning.

Present tense

Writing that talks about something that is happening now, or that happens all of the time.

Punctuation

Symbols which make your writing clearer. For example, full stops and capital letters.

Purpose

The reason why a text has been written.

Report

A text that gives the reader information about something. For example, an accident report.

Sign-off

A phrase used to end a letter or an email. For example, 'Yours faithfully' or 'Best wishes'.

Silent letters

Letters in a word which you can't hear when the word is said out loud. For example the letter 'k' in the word 'knew'.

Singular

The form of a word that refers to only one of something.

Subheading

A title for one section of a text. A subheading usually says what the section is about.

Suffixes

Letters added to the end of a word which change the word's meaning.

Text

A piece of writing. For example a letter, a report or an email.

Verb

A doing or being word. For example 'run' or 'was'.

Webpage

A type of text found on a website.

Entry Level 3 Word List

There are certain words you need to know

1) The words in the list below could come up in the **reading test**, the **spelling part** of the **writing test** or **both** at Entry Level 3.

2) It's important that you know what these words **mean** and how to **spell** them.

according	communicate	experience	popular
achieve	community	experiment	position
actual	competition	explanation	purpose
although	condemn	famous	qualification
appear	correspond	fasten	qualify
apply	cough	frequently	receive
appreciate	criticise	guarantee	recent
attach	crumb	increase	regular
autumn	curiosity	island	rough
available	debt	knee	scheme
average	definite	knife	sugar
bargain	describe	knot	suppose
bomb	determined	knowledge	therefore
borough	develop	listen	thorough
bought	dictionary	measure	though
brought	doubt	medicine	thumb
cause	ease	minute	tough
centre	education	occasion	treasure
certain	enough	opposite	various
climb	equip	ought	whistle
college	especially	particular	
column	excellent	picture	
committee	exercise	pleasure	

There's more information about the word list on page 95.

Watch out for these homophones

1) Homophones are words that **sound the same**, but are **spelt** differently and **mean** different things.

2) The homophones below could come up in the **reading test**, the **spelling part** of the **writing test** or **both**.

3) Make sure you understand the **difference** between them.

Turn to pages 84-87 for more on homophones.

accept / except	farther / father	mail / male	
aloud / allowed	groan / grown	meat / meet	
berry / bury	guessed / guest	missed / mist	scene / seen
brake / break	heel / he'll	passed / past	steal / steel
desert / dessert	knot / not	peace / piece	weather / whether
fair / fare	led / lead	plain / plane	who's / whose

You may be asked about Entry Level 1 and Entry Level 2 words

1) Words from the **Entry Level 1** and **Entry Level 2** word lists could also come up in the test, so it's **worth learning** them as well.

2) Here are some of the more **difficult words** from these lists:

address	double	naughty	something
among	eighteen	notice	special
answer	eighty	one / won	sugar
bare / bear	extreme	position	thirty
beautiful	forty	possess	thought
believe	grammar	potatoes	through
blew / blue	hear / here	pressure	Thursday
breathe	height	probably	Tuesday
business	imagine	quarter	Wednesday
calendar	know	quiet / quite	weigh
caught	knowledge	Saturday	weight
complete	machine	school	
country	material	someone	

Index